Primary Sources 1:
World War I

This collection is one part of an Open University integrated teaching system and the selection is therefore related to other material available to students. It is designed to evoke the critical understanding of students.

AA312 Total War and Social Change: Europe 1914–1955

Book 1 *Europe in 1914*
Book 2 *The Impact of World War I*
Book 3 *Between Two Wars*
Book 4 *The Impact of World War II*
Book 5 *Retrospect: War and Change in Europe 1914–1955*

Other material associated with the course

Primary Sources 1: World War I, eds Arthur Marwick and Wendy Simpson, Open University, 2000

Primary Sources 2: Interwar and World War II, eds Arthur Marwick and Wendy Simpson, Open University, 2000

Secondary Sources, eds Arthur Marwick and Wendy Simpson, Open University, 2000

Total War and Historical Change: Europe 1914–1955, eds Clive Emsley, Arthur Marwick and Wendy Simpson, Open University Press, 2000 (Course Reader)

J. M. Roberts, *Europe 1880–1945*, Longman, 2001 (third edition) (Set Book)

1

Primary Sources 1: World War I

Edited by Arthur Marwick and Wendy Simpson

This publication forms part of an Open University course: AA312 *Total War And Social Change: Europe 1914–1955*. Details of this and other Open University courses can be obtained from the Course Reservations Centre, PO Box 724, The Open University, Milton Keynes MK7 6ZS, United Kingdom: tel. +44 (0)1908 653231, e-mail ces-gen@open.ac.uk

Alternatively, you may visit the Open University website at http://www.open.ac.uk where you can learn more about the wide range of courses and packs offered at all levels by the Open University.

For availability of this or other components, contact Open University Worldwide Ltd, The Berrill Building, Walton Hall, Milton Keynes MK7 6AA, United Kingdom: tel. +44 (0)1908 858785; fax +44 (0)1908 858787; e-mail ouwenq@open.ac.uk; website http://www.ouw.co.uk

First published 2000. Reprinted 2002

Edited, designed and typeset by The Open University

Printed and bound in the United Kingdom by The Alden Group, Oxford

ISBN 0 7492 85532

Cover illustration: Lina von Schauroth, *Emperor's and People's Thank Offering*, 76.3 × 50.8 cm. Imperial War Museum, London.

1.2

28381B/aa312ps1i1.2

PREFACE

Primary sources are the raw material of history. The subject of total war and social change, an absolutely essential one in the study of twentieth-century European history, gives rise to many vigorous debates. Did the wars have significant social consequences? What is the relationship between the First World War and the Russian, Austrian and German revolutions? Do wars lower or improve the status of women? What is the relationship between war and the arts? Did total war produce mass society, or was mass society produced by total war?

These debates can be followed in the writings of historians, but they should also be studied from the primary sources. In all their variety - in this book are reproduced extracts from diaries, letters, social surveys, political programmes, local and national government documents, international treaties, novels and poems, newspaper reports, cost of living statistics – primary sources bring students and general readers directly into contact with the activities historians go through in producing history.

This collection, together with its companion volume *Primary Sources 2: Interwar and World War II*, is designed to accompany the Open University course AA312, *Total War and Social Change: Europe 1914–1955,* but it will prove of immense value to anyone interested in twentieth-century European history, over which two cataclysmic wars have had a profound influence.

The documents in this volume have been divided into two sections, which correspond to the first two books of the course. Although the documents are of many types and relate to many different topics – political, economic, diplomatic, cultural, and social – there is no sub-organization within these sections. Indeed, the extracts have been arranged in the order in which they are used within the Open University course. This means that they can be approached without any deep preconceptions about which particular topic any of the texts relates to. In fact, depending on the questions asked, primary sources can suggest an amazing range of answers. This method of ordering the documents also results in some fascinating juxtapositions – poems with political programmes, personal reminiscences with international treaties.

The extracts have been selected (and sometimes translated) by members of the course team responsible for *Total War and Social Change.*

ARTHUR MARWICK

WENDY SIMPSON

Acknowledgements

Grateful acknowledgement is made to the following sources for permission to reproduce material in this book:

Document I.8: Clough, S. B. and Saladine, S. (eds) (1968) *A History of Modern Italy: Documents, Reading and Commentary,* Columbia University Press. Copyright © Columbia University Press. Used by permission; *Documents I.9,1.10,1.11:* Excerpts from *Imperial Russia, A Source Book 1900-1817* by Basil Dymtryshyn, copyright © 1967 by Holt, Rinehart and Winston, Inc., reprinted by permission of the publisher; *Document I.15:* Rohl, J. G. C. (1994) 'Admiral von Muller's diary entry of 8th December, 1912', in Cole, T. F. (trans.), *The Kaiser and his Court, Wilhelm II and the Government of Germany,* Cambridge University Press.

Every effort has been made to trace all the copyright owners, but if any has been inadvertently overlooked, the publishers will be pleased to make the necessary arrangements at the first opportunity.

Contents

Preface 5

PART I **11**

I.1 H. V. S. Nisbett, from 'Diaries and memories of the Great War' 13

I.2 From the papers of F. L. Goldthorpe (*c.* 1934) 13

I.3 Extracts from letters to the producers of the BBC television series 'The Great War' (written in July 1963) 14

I.4 Protest against the war 16

I.5 Dr Professor E. Noseda, 'Social insurance' (1913) 18

I.6 William Le Queux, from *The Invasion of 1910* (1906) 19

I.7 Friedrich Bernhardi, from *Germany and the Next War* (1912) 19

I.8 Giovanni Giolitti, 'Ministerial report to the King at the end of the parliamentary session, February 8, 1909' 20

I.9 'The fundamental laws of Imperial Russia, 1906' 22

I.10 'Programme of the Russian Social Democratic Workers' Party (Bolsheviks)' (Aug. 1903) 29

I.11 'Programme of the Russian Constitutional Democratic Party (Kadets)' (1905) 34

I.12 From the British National Insurance Act (16 Dec. 1911) 39

I.13 From the Treaty of Versailles (1919) 45

I.14 Memorandum by Sir Eyre Crowe: 'The aims of German policy' (1907) 52

I.15 Admiral von Müller's (Chief of the Imperial Naval Cabinet) diary entry (8 Dec. 1912) 54

I.16 Count Szögyény (Austro-Hungarian Ambassador to Berlin) to Count Berchtold (Austro-Hungarian Foreign Minister) (5 July 1914) 55

I.17 Telegram from Sir Edward Grey (British Foreign Secretary) to Sir Edward Goschen (British Ambassador in Berlin) (31 July 1914) 56

I.18 Memorandum of Prince Karl Max Lichnowsky (1914) 57

PART II **59**

II.1 From Bethmann's Memorandum: 'Provisional notes on the direction of our policy on the conclusion of peace' (9 Sept. 1914) 61

II.2 From 'The Peace Proposal: letter from Bethmann Hollweg to Mr Joseph Clark Grew (Chargé d'Affaires) of the United States of America (12 Dec. 1916) 62

II.3 First talk with General Ludendorff (16 Feb. 1917) 63

II.4 'Programme of the Union of Economic Interests' [a French employers' organization] (7 April 1919) 64

II.5 Memorandum of the Neukölln Municipal Council to the War Food Department (3 Dec. 1917) 65

II.6 From the Care of Mothers and Young Children Act (London, 1915) 69

II.7 Report of a schoolmaster from Mazerolles, Charente (1915–16) 69

II.8 Department of Charente: the cost of living (price changes in basic commodities, in francs) (15 Feb. 1920) 70

II.9 Dragolioub Yovanovitch, from *The Economic and Social Effects of the War in Serbia (1929)* 71

II.10 Entries from the journal of Brand Whitlock (1916) 71

II.11 Report on British servants, *Bristol Evening News* (19 Feb. 1919) 73

II.12 Wilfred Owen, 'Strange meeting' (1918) 74

II.13 Henri Barbusse, from *Under Fire* (1915) 75

II.14 Erich Maria Remarque, from *All Quiet on the Western Front* (1929) 78

II.15 'The programme of the Progressive Bloc' (25 Aug. 1915) 79

II.16 Paul Miliukov, extracts from a speech in the *Duma* (1 Nov. 1916) 81

II.17 Nicholai Markov, extract from a speech in the *Duma* (3 Nov. 1916) 82

II.18 Vladimir Purishkevich, extract from a speech in the *Duma* (19 Nov. 1916) 82

II.19 'The proclamation of the provisional government' (1 March 1917) 84

II.20 'Order No. 1' (1 March 1917) from The Petrograd Soviet of Workers and Soldiers' Deputies 85

II.21 'Declaration of the Kronstadt soldiers' (1 March 1921) 86

II.22 'Kronstadt sailors' appeal' (8 March 1921) 87

II.23 'The *Reichstag* resolution of 19 July 1917' 89

II.24 Extract from the diary of Hans Peter Hanssen (Nov. 1918) 90

II.25 From a report by Herr von Tschirschky, German Ambassador in Vienna (Sept. 1916) 92

PART I

I.1 H. V. S. Nisbet, from 'Diaries and memories of the Great War'

Several of us said good-bye to Marlborough at the end of July 1914, fully expecting to be back again in September ... My age then was not quite seventeen and a quarter ... Like multitudes of other young men, I became filled with a passionate desire to take part in [the war]. I drank in everything that was said or written by statesmen, ministers of the Church and newspapers about the nobility of our ideals and the righteousness of our Cause. It wasn't a matter of 'our Country, right or wrong'. Our country was 100 per cent right and Germany 100 per cent wrong. We were fighting to uphold the principles of justice and freedom, and international morality, and to smash Kaiserism and German militarism ... We had been taught to worship God one day a week but to worship Country and Empire seven days a week. The British Empire was the greatest empire the world had ever known, and its greatness was due to the superior qualities of the British. Foreigners weren't cast in the same mould.

(H. V. S. Nisbet, '*Diaries and memories of the Great War*', Imperial War Museum, ref: 78/3/1)

I.2 From the papers of F. L. Goldthorpe (*c*.1934)

Why did I join the army in 1914? How many give a concise honest answer to that question twenty years afterwards, and say that they enlisted for any one reason. Probably a glance through their old letters sent home at that time may give an impression of patriotic fervour, but was it fervour or fever?

On the day when England declared war on Germany, we (the family) had gone to Lancaster from Morecambe and saw the Territorials mobilised there. I remember marching alongside them, stirred like most of the onlookers by the noise of the bugles, and the electric atmosphere of that August day. Possibly I got bit with the fever germ then. Our folks always said so, and although I knew there were strong reasons why I should not leave business, I was pretty restless for the next few weeks.

During this time I was subjected to a continual bombardment of skilled propaganda from the War Office, newspapers, friends who had joined up, recruiting meetings, and even pulpits. The occupants of the latter would have served their cause much better by remaining silent. The accusing finger of Kitchener stabbed me at every bill-posting, and tales of German atrocities and stricken Belgium dinned into my ears daily. I suppose it was a combination of these many urgings which sent me to the local drill hall on November 15th. My age then was seventeen and a half. My parents made no objection to my going, beyond advising me to wait till I was old enough. I forget how I got over the age difficulty on enlisting, and presume I must have appeared big enough.

(Papers of F. L. Goldthorpe, *c*.1934, Imperial War Museum, p.113)

I.3 Extracts from letters to the producers of the BBC television series 'The Great War' (written in July 1963)

Extract (a)

I was born on March 5th 1896 leaving school at age 14. I had a very happy school life but my family were very poor. So my only prospects on leaving school was to find work as soon as possible. I did, starting at a flour factory where they made assorted cake mixtures, bun flour, etc.

Working hours 6 a.m. until 6 p.m. Saturdays 6 a.m. until 2 p.m. half hour for breakfast break and one hour for dinner.

The factory being within walking distance I had my meals at home. If I wanted to go footballing, it was direct from work.

I stayed there until after breakfast on the morning of September 7th 1914. Incidentally my wages [were] about twelve shillings per week.

Returning to work on said morning I met a neighbour's son and we decided to enlist which we did at Camberwell [in south-east London] Town Hall. We joined the 6th Battalion Dorset Regiment and the same morning marched away with a few hundred others ... along with us marched wives, mothers and girlfriends, not many fathers. They were working or serving.

(James H. Ellis)

Extract (b)

With some of my pals I volunteered when eighteen years old, to join ... our local infantry Regiment in Birkenhead, 4th Battalion the Cheshire Regiment.

The declaration of war, on 4.8.1914 seemed to us to be the only effective course to protect the trade interest of the nation and counteracting the unemployment caused by the dumping of cheap German manufactured goods.

(G. W. Evans)

Extract (c)

It was Saturday 1st August 1914. I, along with some friends, had returned to Aberdeen after a cycling holiday, to be greeted by newsboy shouts of 'Great European War Clouds. War imminent'.

Of course, we had previously heard of the assassination of Crown Prince Ferdinand in Bosnia, but never, for a moment, dreamt that this foul deed was the go-ahead signal for the greatest and most bloody war of all times ...

There was little excitement among the general public during the first days of the war. It took some time for the gravity of the situation to sink in. The recruiting authorities, however, became increasingly active, so that within a month of the declaration of war every youth in the country was made aware of his importance as a serviceable unit for the cause of King and Country. Thus on the 4th of September 1914 I, along with my chum, joined the 2nd Highland Field Co. Royal Engineers at Aberdeen ...

I had no real patriotic ideals, but I liked the life, the open air and the exercise, in contrast to the hum-drum, closed in atmosphere of the factory; besides, the prospect of adventure was alluring.

(William M. Fraser)

Extract (d)

On the 19th September about a dozen clerks downed pens and walked out of a large City business firm to enlist in a City of London Regt. in Farringdon Road. This movement was very much resented by the office manager who could foresee nothing but chaos that would follow by such a depletion of his staff. Incidentally this action was immediately followed by quite a number of warehousemen.

(Bertram C. Glover)

Extract (e)

I joined the Army as a volunteer in Kitchener's Army at the age of nineteen and eleven months – after having fought hard against the stubbornness of a government department to let six of their staff – (Welshmen from Cardiff) – to join to 'fight for freedom'. This was not a sentimental whim; we were genuinely moved by the raping of Belgium by the Hun. The big menacing finger of Kitchener from our hoardings had not yet been devised. It is possible his finger did later move those who could not make up their minds.

After three weeks of wrangling with the government department, which should in all conscience have been the first to allow their men to join, we were given permission. Certain regiments, such as the Welsh regiments, were not yet open for recruits. Queues outside recruiting offices in the city were tediously lengthy and men were in a hurry. And as we could not wait we decided to go to Penarth (in 1914 a small seaside town 5 miles from Cardiff), the home of one of the six, and who, because of his seniority and wisdom (he was 29) also became our spokesman. He was also a fluent English speaker.

I wore pince-nez: this worried the other five who were anxious we should keep together. On the train journey from Cardiff to Penarth (there were no buses then) they advised me to take off my pince-nez to get accustomed to the air and the general atmosphere. All the way they became my mentors by asking me how many cows and how many sheep I could see in the surrounding fields (since built over).

And we strode into the recruiting office, having put away my glasses. We were received by two stern sergeants in a tiny, untidy office on the first floor of a building no longer identifiable. We had already decided we should like to join the 21st Lancers. It sounded grandiloquent and presented to us a picture of well-upholstered recruits in the resplendent uniform of a lancer charging, in due course, like the German Uhlans of whom we had read and cursed for their inhumanity.

(W. R. Owen)

Extract (f)

On the 5th August 1914, when I was a raw lad of 18, times were hard in my home town of Bradford, and I, in common with many others was working only three days a week and having three days dole money.

Idling the time away one day, my friends and I were discussing the dreariness of unemployment when someone suggested we should enlist and the Hussars was mentioned. This sounded to me like a glorious adventure...

(Thomas E. Peers)

Extract (g)

I returned to my old farm at Akenfield for 11s. a week, but I was unsettled. When the farmer stopped my pay because it was raining and we couldn't thrash, I said to my seventeen-year-old mate, 'Bugger him. We'll go and join the army'.

(Leonard Thompson to Ronald Blythe, quoted in Peter Vansittart (ed.) *Voices from the Great War*, 1981), The Imperial War Museum ref: IWM BBC/GW.

I.4 Protest against the war

(a) 'Dominance of Russia or Germany', letter to *The Times* (1 Aug. 1914)

Views of Mr Norman Angell to the Editor of *The Times*

Sir, – A nation's first duty is to its own people.

We are asked to intervene in the Continental war because unless we do so we shall be 'isolated'. The isolation which will result for us if we keep out of this war is that, while other nations are torn and weakened by war, we shall not be, and by that fact might conceivably for a long time be the strongest Power in Europe, and, by virtue of our strength and isolation, its arbiter, perhaps, to useful ends.

We are told that if we allow Germany to become victorious she would be so powerful as to threaten our existence by the occupation of Belgium, Holland, and possibly the North of France. But, as your article of today's date so well points out, it was the difficulty that Germany found in Alsace-Lorraine which prevented her from acting against us during the South African War. If one province, so largely German in its origin and history, could create this embarrassment, what trouble will not Germany pile up for herself if she should attempt the absorption of a Belgium, a Holland, and a Normandy? She would have created for herself embarrassments compared with which Alsace and Poland would be a trifle: and Russia, with her 160,000,000, would in a year or two be as great a menace to her as ever.

The object and effect of our entering into this war would be to ensure the victory of Russia and her Slavonic allies. Will a dominant Slavonic federation of, say, 200,000,000 autocratically governed people, with a very rudimentary civilization, but heavily equipped for military aggression, be a less dangerous factor in Europe than a dominant Germany of 65,000,000, highly civilized and mainly given to the arts of trade and commerce?

The last war we fought on the Continent was for the purpose of preventing the growth of Russia. We are now asked to fight one for the purpose of promoting it. It is now universally admitted that our last Continental war – the Crimean War – was a monstrous error and miscalculation. Would this intervention be any wiser or likely to be better in its results?

On several occasions Sir Edward Grey has solemnly declared that we are not bound by any agreement to support France, and there is certainly no moral obligation on the part of the English people so to do. We can best serve civilization, Europe – including France – and ourselves by remaining the one power in Europe that has not yielded to war madness.

This, I believe, will be found to be the firm conviction of the overwhelming majority of the English people.

Yours faithfully,
Norman Angell
4, King's Bench-Walk, Temple, E.C., July 31.

(*The Times*, 1 August 1914)

(b) 'Scholars' protest against war with Germany', from *The Times* (1 Aug. 1914)

Peace manifestos were issued from various quarters yesterday. A number of university professors and others, who state that they all in different ways enjoy the friendship and co-operation of German colleagues, sign the following protest and appeal for the support of English scholars:

> We regard Germany as a nation leading the way in the Arts and Sciences, and we have all learnt and are learning from German scholars. War upon her in the interest of Serbia and Russia will be a sin against civilization. If by reason of honourable obligations we be unhappily involved in war, patriotism might still our mouths, but at this juncture we consider ourselves justified in protesting against being drawn into the struggle with a nation so near akin to our own, and with whom we have so much in common.

(*The Times*, 1 August 1914)

(c) 'A socialist demonstration', from *The Times* (1 Aug. 1914)

The socialists decided at a meeting at the House of Commons yesterday to hold a demonstration in Trafalgar Square tomorrow. A resolution similar in terms to one passed by the British section of the International Socialist Bureau, under the chairmanship of Mr Keir Hardie, will be moved at the meeting. That resolution is in the following terms:

That we view with serious alarm the prospect of a European war into which every European power will be dragged owing to secret alliances and understandings which, in their origin, were never sanctioned by the nations, nor are even now communicated to them.

We stand by the efforts of the international working class movement to unite the workers of the nations concerned in their efforts to prevent their Governments from entering upon war, as expressed in the resolution passed by the International Socialist Bureau.

We protest against any step being taken by the Government of this country to support Russia, either directly or in consequence of any understanding with France as being not only offensive to the political traditions of the country but disastrous to Europe, and declare that as we have no interest, direct or indirect, in threatened quarrels which may result from the action to Austria in Serbia, the Government of Great Britain should decline to engage in war, but should confine itself to efforts to bring about peace as speedily as possible.

(*The Times*, 1 August 1914)

I.5 Dr Professor E. Noseda, 'Social insurance' (1913)

A Optional Insurance

Title I

Constitution and administration of the fund

1. There is instituted a national benevolent fund for the incapacity or old age of workers. This constitutes an autonomous corporation, with its central office in Rome, and with secondary, departmental, provincial or communal offices, according to the rules set out in the governing statute of the fund, approved by royal decree and passed by the Council of Social Insurance and the Council of State.

   As an autonomous body the said national benevolent fund has an agency and its own administration, distinct from that of the State, which is prohibited from taking on any other responsibilities or duties outside what is laid down in the following articles.

...

Title IV

Joining the Fund

13. Those who may join the national benevolent fund are Italian citizens of both sexes who render service of work by the day or who in general do work that is predominantly manual for third parties or also on their own account, provided that, in this latter case, they do not pay, in whatever form, taxes to the State higher than 30 lire a year.

Married women may join without needing the consent of their husband, and minors without the authorization of whoever exercises the paternal authority or guardianship ... .

(*Manuale di legislazione sociale italiana*, Milan, 1913; trans. A. Marwick)

I.6 William Le Queux, from *The Invasion of 1910* (1906)

'The Surprise'

... In a moment the superintendent had taken the operator's seat, adjusted the ear-piece, and was in conversation with Ipswich. A second later he was speaking with the man who had actually witnessed the cutting of the trunk line.

While he was thus engaged an operator at the farther end of the switchboard suddenly gave vent to a cry of surprise and disbelief.

'What do you say, Beccles? Repeat it,' he asked excitedly. Then a moment later he shouted aloud:

'Beccles says that German soldiers – hundreds of them – are pouring into the place! The Germans have landed at Lowestoft, they think.'

All who heard these ominous words sprang up dumbfounded, staring at each other. The assistant-superintendent dashed to the operator's side and seized his apparatus.

'Halloa – halloa, Beccles! Halloa – Halloa – Halloa!'

The response was some gruff words in German, and sounds of scuffling could distinctly be heard. Then all was silent ... .

But what held everyone breathless in the trunk telephone headquarters was that the Germans had actually effected the surprise landing that had so often been predicted by the military critics; that England on that quiet September Sunday morning had been attacked. England was actually invaded. It was incredible!

(*The Invasion of 1910*, Eveleigh Nash, 1906, ch. 1, pp.9–10)

I.7 Friedrich Bernhardi, from *Germany and the Next War* (1912)

The openly declared aims of England and France are the more worthy of attention since an *entente* prevails between the two countries. In the face of these claims the German nation, from the standpoint of its importance to civilization, is fully entitled not only to demand a place in the sun, as Prince Bulow used modestly to express it, but to aspire to an adequate share in the sovereignty of the world far beyond the limits of its present sphere of influence. But we can only reach this goal by so amply securing our position in Europe that it can never again be questioned. Then only we need no longer fear that we shall be opposed by stronger opponents whenever we take part in international politics. We shall then be able to exercise our forces freely in fair rivalry with the other world Powers, and secure to German nationality and German spirit throughout the globe that high esteem which is due to them ...

We have long underestimated the importance of colonies. Colonial possessions which merely serve the purpose of acquiring wealth, and are only used for economic ends, while the owner-State does not think of colonizing in any form of raising the position of the aboriginal population in the economic or social scale, are unjustifiable and immoral, and can never be held permanently...

We are already suffering severely from the want of colonies to meet our requirements. They would not merely guarantee a livelihood to our growing working population, but would supply raw materials and foodstuffs, would buy goods, and open a field of activity to that immense capital of intellectual labour forces which is today unproductive in Germany, or is in the service of foreign interests. We find throughout the countries of the world German merchants, engineers, and men of every profession, employed actively in the service of foreign masters, because German colonies, when they might be profitably engaged, do not exist. In the future, however, the importance of Germany will depend on two points: firstly, how many millions of men in the world speak German? Secondly, how many of them are politically members of the German Empire?

(*Germany and the Next War*, trans. Allen H. Powles, Edward Arnold, 1912)

I.8 Giovanni Giolitti, 'Ministerial report to the King at the end of the parliamentary session, February 8, 1909'

Your Majesty!

The Legislature that has now come to an end had brought to completion reforms of truly exceptional importance in almost all branches of legislative activity. In execution of the programme presented by the government before the last general election [1904], the state assumed the management of the principal rail networks, including 13,200 kilometres of rail previously managed by private concerns. By purchasing the Southern railways the state became proprietor of all the principal rail networks. Two subsequent laws authorized the expenditure of 910 million lire for the proper reorganization of the rail lines that had been nationalized. The beneficial effect derived from this improved state of the railways is now being seen in our success in meeting the needs of traffic that has increased beyond all expectations ...

Public works projects, which so greatly promote the development of national wealth, were given a strong stimulus. We note the following: the law of July 12, 1906, authorizing the construction of supplementary rail lines in Sicily; the law which authorized construction of railways and many other public works in Basilicata and Calabria; the law of July 14, 1907, for new port facilities which was the most complete law ever voted by the Italian Parliament in this field; the law of July 12, 1908, which authorized the construction of new railways with an estimated expenditure of 600 million lire; and the bill for internal water transportation already submitted to the Chamber and to be resubmitted to the new Chamber.

Systematic reforms of the public services also figured large in our legislative efforts. We note changes in the judiciary system: a law regulating the operation of the magistracy and fixing the legal tenure and other rights of magistrates; a law reordering the offices of court clerks and secretaries as well as the operation of administrative justice. We note also the law on the legal status of secondary school teachers and of civil service employees; a law for the furtherance of elementary school education; a bill on university professors already submitted to the Chamber and to be resubmitted to the new Chamber; a law reorganizing the services in the fine arts; a bill already approved by the Chamber safeguarding our artistic heritage; numerous laws on the reorganization of various services in the navy; a new law on recruitment for the army; and a law appropriating funds for extraordinary military expenditures in defence of the state ... .

The past legislature's activity was even more intense in the field of social reforms. A comprehensive body of laws has assured all workers of a weekly day of rest; the Fund for Workers' Disability and Old Age Pensions has been strengthened and put on a more solid footing; nightwork in bakeries was abolished; laws regulating woman and child labour were improved; conditions of labour in rice cultivation were improved; two laws were passed greatly facilitating and subsidizing the construction of low-income housing; the rehabilitation of prison convicts was made easier and more speedy; low interest loans were made more accessible ... to communes for the construction of aqueducts and other public health installations; a bill was presented to help solve the very grave problem of abandoned children; ... and two parliamentary enquiries were ordered on the condition of land workers in the south and Sicily, as well as of miners in Sardinia. The results of these enquiries will make it possible for us to take effective measures on behalf of such large groups of workers.

Finally, during the course of the past legislature a large number of laws were passed to meet the special needs in several regions of the country ...

This rapid sketch of the more important laws voted by Parliament shows how worthily it has rewarded the country's trust. As a whole these laws are the reflection of a policy of peace, freedom, work, and social justice. We believe that this policy should be continued with ever increasing firmness and vigour so that our country may rapidly approach that goal which was and is the ideal of all who love Italy. That this ideal may be reached by persevering along the road we have followed is proved in an evident fashion by the great progress Italy has made during the last few years.

(Clough, S. B. and Saladine, S. (eds) *A History of Modern Italy: Documents, Reading and Commentary*, New York, Columbia University Press, 1968, pp.275–7)

I.9 'The fundamental laws of Imperial Russia, 1906'

1. The Russian state is unified and indivisible.
2. The Grand Duchy of Finland, while comprising an inseparable part of the Russian state, is governed in its internal affairs by special decrees based on special legislation.
3. The Russian language is the official state language and its use is obligatory in the Army, the Fleet, and in all state and public institutions. The use of local languages and dialects in state and public institutions is determined by special laws.

Chapter I The Essence of the Supreme Autocratic Power

4. The All-Russian Emperor possesses the supreme autocratic power. Not only fear and conscience, but God himself, commands obedience to his authority.
5. The person of the Sovereign Emperor is sacred and inviolable.
6. The same supreme autocratic power belongs to the Sovereign Empress, should the order of succession to the throne pass to a female line; her husband, however, is not considered a sovereign; except for the title, he enjoys the same honours and privileges reserved for the spouses of all other sovereigns.
7. The Sovereign Emperor exercises the legislative authority jointly with the State Council and the State *Duma*.
8. The Sovereign Emperor enjoys the legislative initiative in all legislative matters. The State Council and the State *Duma* may examine the Fundamental State Laws only on his initiative.
9. The Sovereign Emperor approves laws; and without his approval no legislative measure can become law.
10. The Sovereign Emperor possesses the administrative power in its totality throughout the entire Russian state. On the highest level of administration his authority is direct; on subordinate levels of administration, in conformity with the law, he determines the degree of authority of subordinate branches and officials who act in his name and in accordance with his orders.
11. As supreme administrator, the Sovereign Emperor, in conformity with the existing laws, issues decrees for the organization and functioning of diverse branches of state administration as well as directives essential for the execution of the laws.
12. The Sovereign Emperor alone is the supreme leader of all foreign relations of the Russian state with foreign countries. He also determines the direction of foreign policy of the Russian state.
13. The Sovereign Emperor alone declares war, concludes peace and negotiates treaties with foreign states.

14. The Sovereign Emperor is the Commander-in-Chief of the Russian Army and of the Fleet. He possesses supreme command over all the land and sea forces of the Russian state. He determines the organization of the Army and of the Fleet, and issues decrees and directives dealing with the distribution of the armed forces, their transfer to a war footing, their training, the duration of service by various ranks of the Army and of the Fleet and all other matters related to the organization of the armed forces and the defence of the Russian state. As supreme administrator, the Sovereign Emperor determines limitation on the rights of residence and the acquisition of immovable property in localities that have fortifications and defensive positions for the Army and the Fleet.
15. The Sovereign Emperor has the power to declare martial law or a state of emergency in localities.
16. The Sovereign Emperor has the right to coin money and to determine its physical appearance.
17. The Sovereign Emperor appoints and dismisses the Chairman of the Council of Ministers, Ministers, and Chief Administrators of various departments, as well as other officials whose appointment or dismissal has not been determined by law.
18. As supreme administrator the Sovereign Emperor determines the scope of activity of all state officials in accordance with the needs of the state.
19. The Sovereign Emperor grants titles, medals and other state distinctions as well as property rights. He also determines conditions and procedure for gaining titles, medals, and distinctions.
20. The Sovereign Emperor directly issues decrees and instructions on matters of property that belongs to him as well as on those properties that bear his name and which have traditionally belonged to the ruling Emperor. The latter cannot be bequeathed or divided and are subject to a different form of alienation. These as well as other properties are not subject to levy or collection of taxes.
21. As head of the Imperial Household, the Sovereign Emperor, in accordance with Regulations on the Imperial Family, has the right to issue regulations affecting princely properties. He also determines the composition of the personnel of the Ministry of the Imperial Household, its organization and regulation, as well as the procedure of its administration.
22. Justice is administered in the name of the Sovereign Emperor in courts legally constituted, and its execution is also carried out in the name of His Imperial Majesty.
23. The Sovereign Emperor has the right to pardon the accused, to mitigate the sentence, and even to completely forgive transgressions; including the right to terminate court actions against the guilty and to free them from trial and punishment. Stemming from royal mercy, he also has the right to commute the official penalty and to generally pardon all exceptional cases that are not subject to general laws, provided such actions do not infringe upon civil rights or the legally protected interests of others.

24. Statutes of the *Svod Zakanov* (Vol. 1, part 1, 1892 edition) on the order of succession to the throne (Articles 3–17), on the coming of age of the Sovereign Emperor, on government and guardianship (Articles 18–30), on the ascension to the throne. and on the oath of allegiance (Articles 31–34 and Appendix V), on the sacred crowning and anointing (Articles 35 and 36), and on the title of His Imperial Majesty and on the State Emblem (Articles 37–39 and Appendix 1), and on the faith (Articles 40–46), retain the force of the Fundamental Laws.
25. The Regulation on the Imperial Family (*Svod Zakanov*, Vol. 1, part 1, 1892 edition, Articles 82–179 and Appendices 11–IV and VI), while retaining the force of the Fundamental Laws, can be changed or amended only by the Sovereign Emperor personally in accordance with the procedure established by him, provided these changes or amendments of these regulations do not infringe upon general laws or provided they do not call for new expenditures from the treasury.
26. Decrees and commands that are issued directly or indirectly by the Sovereign Emperor as supreme administrator are implemented either by the Chairman of the Council of Ministers, or a subordinate minister, or a department head, and are published by the Governing Senate.

Chapter II Rights and Obligations of Russian subjects

27. Conditions for acquiring rights of Russian citizenship, as well as its loss, are determined by law.
28. The defence of the Throne and of the Fatherland is a sacred obligation of every Russian subject. The male population, irrespective of social status, is subject to military service determined by law.
29. Russian subjects are obliged to pay legally instituted taxes and dues and also to perform other obligations determined by law.
30. No one shall be subjected to persecution for a violation of the law except as prescribed by the law.
31. No one can be detained for investigation otherwise than prescribed by law.
32. No one can be tried and punished other than for criminal acts considered under the existing criminal laws, in force during the perpetration of these acts, provided newly enacted laws do not exclude the perpetrated criminal acts from the list of crimes.
33. The dwelling of every individual is inviolable. Breaking into a dwelling without the consent of the owner and search and seizure are allowed only in accordance with the legally instituted procedures.
34. Every Russian subject has the right to freely select his place of dwelling and profession, to accumulate and dispose of property, and to travel abroad without any hindrance. Limits on these rights are determined by special laws.
35. Private property is inviolable. Forcible seizure of immovable property, should state or public need demand such action, is permissible only upon just and decent compensation.

36. Russian subjects have the right to organize meetings that are peaceful, unarmed, and not contrary to the law. The law determines the conditions of meetings, rules governing their termination, as well as limitations on places of meetings.
37. Within the limits determined by law everyone can express his thoughts orally or in writing, as well as distribute these thoughts through publication or other means.
38. Russian subjects have the right to organize societies and unions for purposes not contrary to the law. Conditions for organization of societies and unions, their activity, terms and rules for acquiring legal rights as well as closing of societies and unions, is determined by law.
39. Russian subjects enjoy freedom of religion. Terms to enjoy this freedom are determined by law.
40. Foreigners living in Russia enjoy the rights of Russian subjects, with limitations established by law.
41. Exceptions to the rules outlined in this chapter include localities where martial law is declared or where there exist exceptional conditions that are determined by special laws.

Chapter III Laws

42. The Russian Empire is governed by firmly established laws that have been properly enacted.
43. Laws are obligatory, without exception, for all Russian subjects and foreigners living within the Russian state.
44. No new law can be enacted without the approval of the State Council and the State *Duma*, and it shall not be legally binding without the approval of the Sovereign Emperor.
45. Should extraordinary circumstances demand, when the State *Duma* is not in session, and the introduction of a measure requires a properly constituted legal procedure, the Council of Ministers will submit such a measure directly to the Sovereign Emperor. Such a measure cannot, however, introduce any changes into the Fundamental Laws, or to the organization of the State Council or the State *Duma*, or to the rules governing elections to the Council or to the *Duma*. The validity of such a measure is terminated if the responsible minister or the head of a special department fails to introduce appropriate legislation in the State *Duma* during the first two months of its session upon reconvening, or if the State *Duma* or the State Council should refuse to enact it into law.
46. Laws issued especially for certain localities or segments of the population are not made void by a new law unless such a voiding is specifically intended.
47. Every law is valid for the future, except in those cases where the law itself stipulates that its force is retroactive or where it states that its intent is to reaffirm or explain the meaning of a previous law.

48. The Governing Senate is the general depository of laws. Consequently, all laws should be deposited in the Governing Senate in the original or in duly authorized lists.
49. Laws are published for general knowledge by the Governing Senate according to established rules and are not legally binding before their publication.
50. Legal decrees are not subject to publication if they were issued in accordance with the rules of the Fundamental Laws.
51. Upon publication, the law is legally binding from the time stipulated by the law itself, or, in the case that such a time is omitted, from the day on which the Senate edition containing the published law is received locally. The law itself may stipulate that telegraph or other media of communication be used to transmit it for execution before its publication.
52. The law cannot be repealed otherwise than by another law. Consequently, until a new law repeals the existing law, the old law retains fully its force.
53. No one can be excused for ignorance of the law once it is duly published.
54. Regulations governing combat, technical, and supply branches of the Armed Forces, as well as rules and orders to institutions and authorized personnel of the military and naval establishments are, as a rule, submitted directly to the Sovereign Emperor upon review by the Military and Admiralty Councils, provided that these regulations, rules, and orders affect primarily the above mentioned establishments, do not touch on matters of general laws, and do not call for new expenditures from the treasury; or, if they call for new expenditure, are covered by expected savings by the Military or Naval Ministries. In cases where the expected saving is insufficient to cover the projected expenditure, submission of such regulations, rules, and orders for the Emperor's approval is permitted only upon first requesting, in a prescribed manner, the necessary appropriation.
55. Regulations governing military and naval courts are issued in accordance with Regulations on Military and Naval Codes.

Chapter IV The State Council, State *Duma*, and the Scope of their Activity

56. The Sovereign Emperor, by a decree, annually convenes the session of the State Council and of the State *Duma*.
57. The Sovereign Emperor determines by a decree the length of the annual session of the State Council and of the State *Duma*, as well as the interval between the sessions.
58. The State Council is composed of members appointed by His Majesty and of elected members. The total number of appointed members of the Council called by the Emperor to deliberate in the Council's proceedings cannot exceed the total number of the elected members of the Council.
59. The State *Duma* consists of members elected by the population of the Russian Empire for a period of five years, on the basis of rules governing elections to the *Duma*.

60. The State Council examines the credentials of its members. Equally, the State *Duma* examines the credentials of its members.
61. The same person cannot serve simultaneously as a member of the State Council and as a member of the State *Duma*.
62. The Sovereign Emperor, by a decree, can replace the elected membership of the State Council with new members before its tenure expires. The same decree sets new elections of members of the State Council.
63. The Sovereign Emperor, by a decree, can dissolve the State *Duma* and release its members from their five-year tenure. The same decree must designate new elections to the State *Duma* and the time of its first session.
64. The State Council and the State *Duma* have equal rights in legislative matters.
65. The State Council and the State *Duma* enjoy the constitutional right to submit proposals to repeal or to amend the existing laws as well as to issue new laws, except the Fundamental Law whose review belongs exclusively to the Sovereign Emperor.
66. The State Council and the State *Duma* have a constitutional right to address questions to Ministers and heads of various departments, who legally are under the jurisdiction of the Governing Senate, on matters that stem from violations of laws by them or by their subordinates.
67. The jurisdiction of the State Council and of the State *Duma* includes those matters that are listed in the Rules of the Council and of the *Duma*.
68. Those legislative measures that are considered and approved by the State *Duma* are then submitted to the State Council for its approval. Those legislative measures that have been initiated by the State Council are reviewed by the Council and, upon approval, are submitted to the *Duma*.
69. Legislative measures that have been rejected either by the State Council or by the State *Duma* are considered defeated.
70. Those legislative measures that have been initiated either by the State Council or by the State *Duma* [and approved by both], but which have failed to gain Imperial approval, cannot be re-submitted for legislative consideration during the same session. Those legislative measures that have been initiated by either the State Council or by the State *Duma* and are rejected by either one of the Chambers, can be resubmitted for legislative consideration during the same session, provided the Emperor agrees to it.
71. Legislative measures that have been initiated in and approved by the State *Duma* and then by the State Council, equally as the legislative measures initiated and approved by the State Council and then by the State *Duma*, are submitted by the Chairman of the State Council to the Sovereign Emperor.
72. Deliberations on the state budget [by the State Council and/or by the State *Duma*] cannot exclude or reduce the set sums for the payment of state debts or other obligations assumed by the Russian state.
73. Revenues, for the maintenance of the Ministry of the Imperial Household, including institutions under its jurisdiction that do not exceed the allocated sum of the state budget for 1906, are not subject to review by either the State Council or the State *Duma*. Equally not subject to review are such changes

in specific revenues as stem from decisions based on Regulations of the Imperial Family that have resulted from internal reorganizations.

74. If the state budget is not appropriated before the appropriation deadline, the budget that had been duly approved in the preceding year will remain in force with only such changes as have resulted from those legislative measures that became laws after the budget was approved. Prior to publication of the new budget, on the decision of the Council of Ministers and rulings of Ministries and Special Departments, necessary funds will be gradually released. These funds will not exceed in their totality during any month, however, one-twelfth of the entire budgetary expenditures.

75. Extraordinary budgetary expenditures for war-time needs and for special preparations preceding a war are unveiled in all departments in accordance with existing law on the decision of highest administration.

76. State loans to cover both the estimated and non-estimated expenditures are contracted according to the system established to determine state budgetary revenues and expenditures. State loans to cover expenditures in cases foreseen in Article 74, as well as loans to cover expenditures stipulated in Article 75, are determined by the Sovereign Emperor as supreme administrator. Time and conditions to contract state loans are determined on the highest level of government.

77. If the State *Duma* fails to act on a proposal submitted to it reasonably in advance on the number of men needed for the Army and the Fleet, and a law on this matter is not ready by May 1, the Sovereign Emperor has the right to issue a decree calling to military service the necessary number of men, but not more than the number called the preceding year.

Chapter V Council of Ministers, Ministers and Heads of Various Departments

78. By law, the Council of Ministers is responsible for the direction and co-ordination of activities of Ministers and Heads of various departments on matters affecting legislation as well as the highest state administration.

79. Ministers and Heads of various departments have the right to vote in the State Council and in the State *Duma* only if they are members of these institutions.

80. Binding resolutions, instructions, and decisions issued by the Council of Ministers, and Ministers and Heads of various departments, as well as by other responsible individuals entitled by law, should not be contrary to existing laws.

81. The Chairman of the Council of Ministers, Ministers, and Heads of various departments, are responsible to the Sovereign Emperor for State administration. Each individual member is responsible for his actions and decisions.

82. For official misconducts in office, the Chairman of the Council of Ministers, Ministers and Heads of various departments are subject to civil and criminal punishment established by law.

(*Imperial Russia, A Source Book 1900–1917*, ed. Basil Dmytryshyn, Hinsdale, Ill., The Dryden Press, 1974, pp.387–93)

I.10 'Programme of the Russian Social Democratic Workers' Party (Bolsheviks)' (Aug. 1903)

The development of exchange has created such close ties among all the peoples of the civilized world that the great proletarian movement toward emancipation was bound to become – and has long since become –international.

Considering itself one of the detachments of the universal army of the proletariat, Russian social democracy is pursuing the same ultimate goal as that for which the social democrats in other countries are striving. This ultimate goal is determined by the nature of contemporary bourgeois society and by the course of its development. The main characteristic of such a society is production for the market on the basis of capitalist production relations, whereby the largest and most important part of the means of production and exchange of commodities belongs to a numerically small class of people, while the overwhelming majority of the population consists of proletarians and semi-proletarians who, by their economic conditions, are forced either continuously or periodically to sell their labour power; that is, to hire themselves out to the capitalists, and by their toil to create the incomes of the upper classes of society.

The expansion of the capitalist system of production runs parallel to technical progress, which, by increasing the economic importance of large enterprises, tends to eliminate the small independent producers, to convert some of them into proletarians, to reduce the socio-economic role of others and, in some localities, to place them in more or less complete, more or less open, more or less onerous dependence on capital.

Moreover, the same technical progress enables the entrepreneurs to utilize to an ever greater extent woman and child labour in the process of production and exchange of commodities. And since, on the other hand, technical improvements lead to a decrease in the entrepreneur's demand for human labour power, the demand for labour power necessarily lags behind the supply, and there is in consequence greater dependence of hired labour upon capital, and increased exploitation of the former by the latter.

Such a state of affairs in the bourgeois countries, as well as the ever growing competition among those countries on the world market, render the sale of goods which are produced in greater and greater quantities ever more difficult. Over-production, which manifests itself in more or less acute industrial crises – which in turn are followed by more or less protracted periods of industrial stagnation – is the inevitable consequence of the development of the productive forces in bourgeois society. Crises and periods of industrial stagnation, in their turn, tend to impoverish still further the small producers, to increase still further the dependence of hired labour upon capital, and to accelerate still further the relative, and sometimes the absolute, deterioration of the condition of the working class.

Thus, technical progress, signifying increased productivity of labour and the growth of social wealth, becomes in bourgeois society the cause of increased social inequalities, of wider gulfs between the wealthy and the poor, of greater insecurity of existence, of unemployment, and of numerous privations for ever larger and larger masses of toilers.

But together with the growth and development of all these contradictions inherent in bourgeois society, there grows simultaneously dissatisfaction with the present order among the toiling and exploited masses; the number and solidarity of the proletarians increases, and their struggle against the exploiters sharpens. At the same time, technical progress, by concentrating the means of production and exchange, by socializing the process of labour in capitalist enterprises, creates more and more rapidly the material possibility for replacing capitalist production relations by socialist ones; that is, the possibility for social revolution, which is the ultimate aim of all the activities of international social democracy as the class conscious expression of the proletarian movement.

By replacing private with public ownership of the means of production and exchange, by introducing planned organization in the public process of production so that the well-being and the many-sided development of all members of society may be insured, the social revolution of the proletariat will abolish the division of society into classes and thus emancipate all oppressed humanity, and will terminate all forms of exploitation of one part of society by another.

A necessary condition for this social revolution is the dictatorship of the proletariat; that is, the conquering by the proletariat of such political power as would enable it to crush any resistance offered by the exploiters. In its effort to make the proletariat capable of fulfilling its great historical mission, international social democracy organizes it into an independent political party in opposition to all bourgeois parties, directs all the manifestations of its class struggle, discloses before it the irreconcilable conflict between the interests of the exploiters and those of the exploited, and clarifies for it the historical significance of the imminent social revolution and the conditions necessary for its coming. At the same time, it reveals to the other sections of the toiling and exploited masses the hopelessness of their condition in capitalist society and the need of a social revolution if they wish to be free of the capitalist yoke. The party of the working class, the social democracy, calls upon all strata of the toiling and exploited population to join its ranks insofar as they accept the point of view of the proletariat.

On the road towards their common final goal, which is determined by the prevalence of the capitalist system of production throughout the civilized world, the social democrats of different countries must devote themselves to different immediate tasks – first, because that system is not everywhere developed to the same degree; and second, because in different countries its development takes place in a different socio-political setting.

In Russia, where capitalism has already become the dominant mode of production, there are still preserved numerous vestiges of the old pre-capitalist order, when the toiling masses were serfs of the landowners, the state, or the sovereign. Greatly hampering economic progress, these vestiges interfere with the many-sided development of the class struggle of the proletariat, help to preserve and strengthen the most barbarous forms of exploitation by the state and the propertied classes of the millions of peasants, and thus keep the whole people in darkness and subjection.

The most outstanding among these relics of the past, the mightiest bulwark of all this barbarism, is the tsarist autocracy. By its very nature it is bound to be hostile to any social movement, and cannot but be bitterly opposed to all the aspirations of the proletariat towards freedom.

By reason of the above, the first and immediate task put before itself by the Russian Social Democratic Workers' Party is to overthrow the tsarist autocracy and to replace it with a democratic republic whose constitution would guarantee the following:

1. The sovereignty of the people; that is, the concentration of all supreme state power in the hands of a legislative assembly, consisting of people's representatives, and forming one chamber.
2. Universal, equal, and direct suffrage for all male and female citizens, twenty years old or over, at all elections to the legislative assembly and to the various local organs of self-government; the secret ballot at elections; the right of every voter to be elected to any representative institution; biennial parliaments; salaries to be paid to the people's representatives.
3. Broad local self-government; home rule for all localities where the population is of a special composition and characterized by special conditions of life.
4. Inviolability of person and dwelling.
5. Unlimited freedom of religion, speech, press, assembly, strikes, and unions.
6. Freedom of movement and occupation.
7. Abolition of classes; equal rights for all citizens, irrespective of sex, religion, race, or nationality.
8. The right of any people to receive instruction in its own language, to be secured by creating schools at the expense of the state and the local organs of self-government; the right of every citizen to use his native language at meetings; the introduction of the use of the native language on a par with the state language in all local, public, and state institutions.
9. The right of self-determination for all nations included in the composition of the state.
10. The right of any person to sue any official before a jury in the regular way.
11. Election of judges by the people.
12. Replacement of the standing army by a general armament of the people.
13. Separation of church and state, and of school and church.
14. Free and compulsory general and professional education for all children of both sexes up to the age of sixteen; provision by the state of food, clothing, and school supplies for poor children.

As a basic condition for the democratization of our state economy the Russian Social Democratic Workers' Party demands the abolition of all indirect taxes and the establishment of a progressive tax on income and inheritances.

In order to safeguard the working class against physical and moral degeneration, as well as to insure the development of its power to carry on the struggle for freedom, the party demands the following:

1. Eight-hour working day for all hired labour.
2. A law providing a weekly uninterrupted forty-two-hour respite for all hired labour, of both sexes, in all branches of the national economy.
3. Complete prohibition of overtime work.
4. Prohibition of night work (from 9 p.m. to 6 a.m.) in all branches of the national economy, with the exception of those in which this is absolutely necessary because of technical considerations approved by labour organizations.
5. Prohibition of the employment of children of school age (up to sixteen) and restriction of the working day of minors (from sixteen to eighteen) to six hours.
6. Prohibition of female labour in those branches of industry which are injurious to women's health; relief from work four weeks before and six weeks after childbirth, with regular wages paid during all this period.
7. Establishment of nurseries for infants and children in all shops, factories, and other enterprises that employ women; permission for freedom of at least a half-hour's duration to be granted at three-hour intervals to all nursing mothers.
8. Old-age state insurance, and insurance against total or partial disability; such insurance to be based on a special fund formed from a tax levied on the capitalists.
9. Prohibition of payment of wages in kind; establishment of regular weekly pay days when all wages shall be paid in money in absolute conformity with all the agreements relating to the hire of workers; wages to be paid during working hours.
10. Prohibition of deductions by employers from workers' wages, on any ground or for any purpose (fines, spoilage, and so forth).
11. Appointment of an adequate number of factory inspectors in all branches of the national economy and extension of their supervision to all enterprises employing hired labour, including government enterprises (domestic service also to be within the sphere of their supervision); appointment of special women inspectors in those industries where female labour is employed; participation of representatives, elected by the workers and paid by the state, in supervising the enforcement of the factory laws, the fixing of wage scales, and in accepting or rejecting the finished products and other results of labour.
12. Control by organs of local self-government, together with representatives elected by the workers, over sanitation in the dwellings assigned to the workers by the employers, as well as over internal arrangements in those dwellings and the renting conditions – in order to protect the workers against the employers' interference with their life and activity as private citizens.

13. Establishment of properly organized sanitary control over all establishments employing hired labour, the medico-sanitary organization to be entirely independent of the employers; in time of illness, free medical aid to be rendered to the workers at the expense of the employers, with the workers retaining their wages.
14. Establishment of criminal responsibility in the case of employers' infringement upon the laws intended to protect the workers.
15. Establishment in all branches of the national economy of industrial courts to be composed of representatives of workers and employers in equal numbers.
16. Imposition upon the organs of local self-government of the duty of establishing employment agencies (labour exchanges) to deal with the hiring of local and out-of-town labour in all branches of industry, and participation of workers' and employers' representatives in their administration.

In order to remove the vestiges of serfdom that fall directly and heavily upon the peasants, and to encourage the free development of the class struggle in the village, the party demands above all:

1. Abolition of redemption payments and quit rents as well as all obligations which presently fall on the peasantry, the tax-paying class.
2. Repeal of all laws which restrict the peasant in disposing of his land.
3. Return to peasants of money collected from them in the form of redemption payments and quit rents; confiscation of monastery and church properties as well as property belonging to princes, government agencies, and members of the royal family; imposition of a special tax on lands of nobles who have sold it on loan terms; transfer of the money thus procured into a special reserve fund to meet cultural and charitable needs of villages.
4. Organization of peasant committees: (a) to return to villages (by means of expropriation ...) those lands which were taken away from the peasants at the emancipation, and which are held by the nobles as a means of enserfment of peasants; (b) to transfer to peasant ownership those lands in the Caucasus which they use now on a temporary basis; (c) to eliminate the remnants of serfdom still in effect in the Urals, the Altai, the Western Provinces, and other parts of the country.
5. Grant to the courts the right to lower unusually high rents and to annul those contracts which contain slave characteristics.

To attain its immediate goals, the Russian Social Democratic Workers' Party will support every opposition and revolutionary movement directed against the existing social and political system in Russia. At the same time it rejects all reformist projects whose aim is to extend or to consolidate bureaucratic-police protection over the toiling classes.

On its own part, the Russian Social Democratic Workers' Party is firmly convinced that a full, consistent, and thorough realization of the indicated political and social changes can only be attained by the overthrow of autocracy and by the convocation of a Constituent Assembly freely elected by the entire people.

(*Imperial Russia, A Source Book 1900–1917*, ed. Basil Dmytryshyn, Hinsdale, Ill., The Dryden Press, 1974, pp.394–9)

I.11 'Programme of the Russian Constitutional Democratic Party (Kadets)' (1905)

I Basic Rights of Citizens

1. All Russian citizens, irrespective of sex, religion, or nationality, are equal before the law. All class distinctions and all limitations of personal and property rights of Poles, Jews, and all other groups of the population, should be repealed.
2. Every citizen is guaranteed freedom of conscience and religion. No persecution for religious beliefs or convictions, or for change or refusal to accept religious indoctrination, can be allowed. The celebration of religious and church ceremonies and the spread of beliefs is free, provided these activities do not include any general transgressions contrary to the criminal code of law. The Orthodox Church and other religions should be freed from state protection.
3. Anyone who wishes to express his thoughts orally or in writing has the right to publish and spread them through printing or any other media. Censorship, both general and special, regardless of its name, must be abolished and cannot be reinstituted. For their oral or written transgressions the guilty ones will answer before the court.
4. All Russian citizens have the right to organize public or private meetings, in dwellings as well as in the open air, to examine any problem they wish.
5. All Russian citizens have the right to organize unions or societies without needing permission for it.
6. The right to petition is granted to every citizen as well as to all groups, unions, gatherings, and so forth.
7. The person and home of every individual should be inviolable. Entering of a private dwelling, search, seizure, and opening of private correspondence, are allowed only in cases permitted by law or on order of the court. Any individual detained in cities or places where courts are located should be freed within twenty-four hours; in other localities of the Empire not later than three days, or be brought before the court. Any detention undertaken illegally, or without proper grounds, gives a detained person the right to be compensated by the state for losses suffered.
8. No one can be subjected to persecution or punishment except on the basis of law by court authorities in a legally constituted court. No extraordinary courts are allowed.
9. Every citizen has freedom of movement and travel abroad. The passport system is abolished.
10. All the above – mentioned rights of citizens must be incorporated into the Constitution of the Russian Empire and be guaranteed by courts.
11. The Constitution of the Russian Empire should guarantee all the minorities inhabiting the Empire, in addition to full civil and political equality enjoyed by all citizens, the right of cultural self-determination, namely: full freedom

of usage of various languages and dialects in public, the freedom to found and maintain educational institutions and meetings of all sorts having as their aim the preservation and development of language, literature and culture of every nationality.

12. Russian language should be the official language of central administration, army, and fleet. The use of local languages alongside the official language in state and public institutions and educational establishments supported by the state or organs of local self-government is determined by general and local laws, and within their competence by the institutions concerned. The population of each locality should be guaranteed education in the native language in elementary schools, and possibly in subsequent education.

II Government Apparatus

13. The constitutional system of the Russian state will be determined by the Constitution.
14. People's representatives are elected by a general, equal, direct and secret ballot, irrespective of their religion, nationality or sex.
    The party allows within its midst a difference of opinion on the question of national representation, consisting of one or two chambers, in which case the second chamber should consist of representatives of the local organs of self-government, organized on the basis of a general vote and spread throughout all of Russia.
15. National representation participates in the realization of legislative power, in the determination of government revenues and expenditures, and in control of the legality and expedience of actions of higher and lower organs of administration.
16. No decision, decree, *ukaz*, order or a similar act not based on the legislative measure of national representation, regardless of its name or place of origin, can have the force of law.
17. A government inventory, which should include all revenues and expenditures of the state, should be established by law, every year. No taxes, dues, and collections for the state, as well as state loans, can be established other than by legislation.
18. Members of national representative assemblies should have the right of legislative initiative.
19. Ministers are responsible to the representatives of the national assembly, and the latter have the right of questioning and interpellation.

III Local Self-Government and Autonomy

20. Local self-government should be extended throughout the entire Russian state.
21. Representatives in the organs of local self-government, being close to the population by virtue of the organization of small self-governing units, should be elected on the basis of universal, equal, direct, and secret ballot, regardless of sex, religion, and nationality, while the assemblies of higher

self-governing units can be selected by lower assemblies. *Gubernia zemstvos* should have the right to enter into temporary or permanent unions among themselves.

22. The competence of the organs of local self-government should include the entire field of local administration, including police, but excluding only those branches of administration which, under the condition of present state life, must be located in the hands of the central government. Organs of the local self-government should receive partial support from sources which now go to the budget of the central government.
23. The activity of representatives of the central government should be limited to supervision of the legality of acts of the organs of local self-government; the final decision on any disputes or doubts is reserved for the courts.
24. Following the establishment of rights of civil freedom and proper representation with constitutional rights for the entire Russian state, there should be opened a legal way within the framework of state legislation for the establishment of local autonomy and *oblast* representative assemblies, with the right to participate in the realization of legislative authority on familiar matters in accordance with the needs of the population.
25. Immediately following the introduction of the imperial democratic government with constitutional rights, there should be established in the Polish kingdom an autonomous administration with a *sejm* [Parliament] elected on the same basis as the state parliament of Russia, preserving its state unity and participation in the central parliament on an equal footing with other parts of the Empire. Frontiers between the Polish kingdom and neighbouring *gubernias* shall be established in accordance with the native population and desires of the local population. In the Polish kingdom there should be instituted national guarantees of civil freedom and rights of nationalities on cultural self-determination as well as protection of the rights of minorities.
26. *Finland.* The Finnish Constitution, which safeguards its special state status, should be fully reinstated. All future measures common to the Empire and the Grand Duchy of Finland should be solved by an agreement between legislative branches of the Empire and the Grand Duchy.

IV Courts

27. All departures from the bases of the Judicial Statute of November 20, 1864, which separated judicial from administrative power (irremovability of judges, independence of courts, and equality of all citizens before the court) as well as the introduction of subsequent novelties are to be abolished ... Courts with class representatives are abolished. Matters of *volost* justice are subject to the competence of an elected justice of the peace. The *volost* court and the institution of *zemskii nachalniks* [land administrators] are abolished. The demand for property qualifications to perform the functions of a Justice of the Peace as well as that of a sworn deputy is abolished. The principle of the unity of appellate court is re-established. Advocacy is organized on the foundation of true self-administration.

28. In addition to this, the aim of penal policy should consist of: (a) unconditional abolishment forever of the death penalty; (b) introduction of conditional conviction; (c) establishment of protection during preliminary investigation; and (d) introduction into court proceedings of controvertible rule.
29. The immediate task centres in the full examination of the criminal code, the annulment of decrees which are contrary to the foundations of political freedom, and the reworking of the project of the civil code.

V Financial and Economic Policy

30. There should be re-examination of government expenditure in order to eliminate unproductive expenses, and to bring about an appreciable increase of state resources for the real needs of the people.
31. The redemption payments should be repealed.
32. There should be replacement of indirect by direct taxes, general lowering of indirect taxes, and gradual repeal of indirect taxes on items of general consumption.
33. There should be a reform of direct taxes on the basis of progressive income, a reform of property taxation, and a progressive tax on inheritance.
34. In conformity with the condition of individual industries there should be a lowering of custom duties in order to cut down the cost of products of general consumption and to improve the technical level of industry and agriculture.
35. Saving banks should be used for the development of small loans.

VI Agrarian Legislation

36. There should be an increase of arable land for that part of the population which works the land with its own labour, namely landless and petty peasants – as well as other peasants by state, princely, cabinet, monastery, and private estates at the state's expense, with private owners being compensated at a fair (not market) price for their land.
37. Expropriated land should be transferred to a state and land reserve. Rules by which the land from this reserve should be given to a needy population (ownership, or personal or communal use, and so forth) should be determined in accordance with peculiarities of land ownership and land usage in different parts of Russia.
38. There should be broad organization of government aid to migration, resettlement, and arrangement of the economic life of peasants. There should be reorganization of the Boundary Office, termination of surveying and introduction of other measures for bringing prosperity to the rural population and improving the rural economy.
39. Legislation dealing with the lease relationship should be promulgated in order to protect the right of tenants and the right to re-lease ... .
40. The existing rules on hiring of agricultural workers should be repealed and labour legislation should be extended to agricultural workers ... .

VII Labour Legislation

41. There should be freedom of labour unions and assemblies.
42. The right to strike should be granted. Punishment for violations of law which occur during or as a result of strikes should be determined in general terms and under no circumstances should be extreme.
43. Labour legislation and independent inspection of labour should be extended to all forms of hired labour; there should be participation of workers' elected representatives in inspections aimed at safeguarding the interests of workers.
44. Legislation should introduce the eight-hour working day. Where possible, this norm should be immediately realized everywhere, and systematically introduced in other industries. Night work and overtime work should be prohibited except where technically and socially indispensable.
45. Protection of female and child labour and the establishment of special measures to protect male labour should be developed in dangerous enterprises.
46. Arbitration offices consisting of an equal number of representatives of labour and capital to regulate all kinds of hiring which are not regulated by labour legislation, and solving of disputes which may arise between workers and employers, should be established.
47. Obligatory state medical care (for a definite period), accident and work-connected illness compensations, which are to be contributed to by the employers, should be established.
48. State old age security and disability allowances for all individuals who make a living by their own work should be introduced.
49. Criminal responsibility for violation of laws dealing with the protection of labour should be established.

VIII Problems for Education

Public education should be founded on freedom, democracy, and decentralisation in order to realize the following goals:

50. The elimination of all restrictions on school admissions based on sex, origin or religion.
51. Freedom of private and public initiative to found and organize all sorts of educational institutions, including education outside the school; freedom of instruction.
52. Better liaison should be organized between various school classes in order to make easier a transfer from one school to another.
53. There should be full autonomy and freedom of instruction in universities and other institutions of higher learning. Their numbers should increase. The fee for attending lectures should be lowered. Institutions of higher learning should organize education to meet the needs of broad layers of society. Students should have freedom to organize themselves.

54. The number of institutions of secondary learning should increase in accordance with public needs; the fee for these should be reduced. Local public institutions should have the right to participate in the formulation of the education curriculum.
55. A universal, free, and obligatory system of education should be introduced in elementary schools. Local self-government should extend material aid to those who need it.
56. Local self-government should organize institutions for the education of the adult population - elementary schools for the adult, as well as public libraries and public universities.
57. Professional education should be developed.

(*Imperial Russia, A Source Book 1900–1917*, ed. Basil Dmytryshyn, Hinsdale, Ill., The Dryden Press, 1974, pp.405–10)

I.12 From the British National Insurance Act (16 Dec. 1911)

Part I National Health Insurance

Insured Persons

1. (1) Subject to the provisions of this Act, all persons of the age of sixteen and upwards who are employed within the meaning of this Part of this Act shall be, and any such persons who are not so employed but who possess the qualifications herein-after mentioned may be, insured in manner provided in this Part of this Act, and all persons so insured (in this Act called 'insured persons') shall be entitled in the manner and subject to the conditions provided in this Act to the benefits in respect of health insurance and prevention of sickness conferred by this Part of this Act.

(2) The persons employed within the meaning of this Part of this Act (in this Act referred to as 'employed contributors') shall include all persons of either sex, whether British subjects or not, who are engaged in any of the employments specified in Part I of the First Schedule to this Act, not being employments specified in Part II of that schedule:

Provided that the Insurance Commissioners herein-after constituted may, with the approval of the Treasury, by a special order made in manner herein-after provided, provide for including amongst the persons employed within the meaning of this Part of the Act any persons engaged in any of the excepted employments specified in Part II of the said schedule either unconditionally or subject to such conditions as may be specified in the order.

(3) The persons not employed within the meaning of this Part of this Act who are entitled to be insured persons include all persons who either:

(a) are engaged in some regular occupation and are wholly or mainly dependent for their livelihood on the earnings derived by them from that occupation; or

(b) have been insured persons for a period of five years or upwards; and the persons possessing such qualifications who become or continue to be insured persons are in this Act referred to as voluntary contributors: provided always that no person whose total income from all sources exceeds one hundred and sixty pounds a year shall be entitled to be a voluntary contributor unless he has been insured under this Part of this Act for a period of five years or upwards.

(4) Except as herein-after provided, nothing in this section shall require or authorise a person of the age of sixty-five or upwards not previously insured under this Part of this Act to become so insured.

2. (1) Where any person employed within the meaning of this Part of this Act proves that he is either:

(a) in receipt of any pension or income of the annual value of twenty-six pounds or upwards not dependent upon his personal exertions; or

(b) ordinarily and mainly dependent for his livelihood upon some other person;

he shall be entitled to a certificate exempting him from the liability to become or to continue to be insured under this Part of this Act.

(2) All claims for exemption shall be made to, and certificates of exemption granted by, the Insurance Commissioners in the prescribed manner and subject to the prescribed conditions, and may be so made and granted before, as well as after, the commencement of this Act: Provided that the regulations of the Insurance Commissioners may provide for claims under this section being made to and certificates granted by approved societies and Insurance Committees herein-after constituted.

Contributions

3. Except as otherwise provided by this Act, the funds for providing the benefits conferred by this Part of this Act and defraying the expenses of the administration of those benefits shall be derived as to seven-ninths (or, in the case of women, three-fourths) thereof from contributions made by or in respect of the contributors by themselves or their employers, and as to the remaining two-ninths (or, in the case of women, one quarter) thereof from moneys provided by Parliament.

4. (1) The contributions payable in respect of employed contributors shall be at the rate specified in Part 1 of the Second Schedule to this Act (herein-after referred to as the employed rate), and shall comprise contributions by the contributors and contributions by their employers at the rates specified in that Part of that schedule, and shall be payable at weekly or other prescribed intervals:

Provided that, in the case of an employed contributor of the age of twenty-one or upwards whose remuneration does not include the provision of board and lodging by the employer and the rate of whose remuneration does not exceed two shillings a working day, such part of the contributions payable in respect of him as is specified in the said schedule shall be paid out of moneys provided by Parliament.

(2) The employer shall, in the first instance, pay both the contributions payable by himself (in this Act referred to as the employer's contributions), and also on behalf of the employed contributor the contributions payable by such contributor, and shall be entitled to recover from the contributor, by deduction from his wages or otherwise the amount of the contributions so paid by him on behalf of the contributor, in accordance with the rules set out in the Third Schedule to this Act.

(3) Contributions in respect of employed contributors shall cease to be payable on their attaining the age of seventy.

(4) The employer of a person who though employed within the meaning of this Part of this Act is not insured under this Part of this Act by reason either:

(a) that, not having previously been an insured person, he has become employed within the meaning of this part of this Act after attaining the age of sixty-five; or

(b) that he has obtained and still holds a certificate of exemption under this Part of this Act;

shall be liable to pay the like contributions as would have been payable as employer's contributions if such person had been an employed contributor, and such contributions shall be carried to such account and dealt with in such manner as may be prescribed by regulations made by the Insurance Commissioners, and those regulations may provide for applying the sums standing to the credit of the account, or any part thereof, for the benefit of any persons in respect of whom contributions have been so paid, in the event of such persons subsequently becoming employed contributors ....

Part II Unemployment Insurance

84. Every workman who, having been employed in a trade mentioned in the Sixth Schedule to this Act (in this Act referred to as 'an insured trade') is unemployed, and in whose case the conditions laid down by this Part of this Act (in this Act referred to as 'statutory conditions') are fulfilled, shall be entitled, subject to the provisions of this Part of this Act, to receive payments (in this Act referred to as 'unemployment benefit') at weekly or other prescribed intervals at such rates and for such periods as are authorised by or under the Seventh Schedule to this Act ....

85. (1) The sums required for the payment of unemployment benefit under this Act shall be derived partly from contributions by workmen in the insured trades and partly from contributions by employers of such workmen and partly from moneys provided by Parliament.

(2) Subject to the provisions of this Part of this Act, every workman employed within the United Kingdom in an insured trade, and every employer of any such workman, shall be liable to pay contributions at the rates specified in the Eighth Schedule to this Act.

(3) Except where the regulations under this Part of this Act otherwise prescribe, the employer shall, in the first instance, be liable to pay both the contribution payable by himself, and also on behalf of and to the exclusion of the workman, the contribution payable by such workman, and subject to such regulations, shall be entitled, notwithstanding the provisions of any Act or any contract to the contrary, to recover from the workman by deductions from the workman's wages or from any other payment due from him to the workman the amount of the contributions so paid by him on behalf of the workman.

(4) Notwithstanding any contract to the contrary, the employer shall not be entitled to deduct from the wages of or other payment due to the workman, or otherwise recover from the workman by any legal process the contributions payable by the employer himself .... .

(6) A contribution shall be made in each year out of moneys provided by Parliament equal to one-third of the total contributions received from employers and workmen during that year, and the sums to be contributed in any year shall be paid in such manner and at such times as the Treasury may determine.

86. The statutory conditions for the receipt of unemployment benefit by any workman are:

(1) That he proves that he has been employed as a workman in an insured trade in each of not less than twenty-six separate calendar weeks in the preceding five years;

(2) That he has made application for unemployment benefit in the prescribed manner, and proves that since the date of the application he has been continuously unemployed;

(3) That he is capable of work but unable to obtain suitable employment;

(4) That he has not exhausted his right to unemployment benefit under this Part of this Act:

Provided that a workman shall not be deemed to have failed to fulfil the statutory conditions by reason only that he has declined:

(a) an offer of employment in a situation vacant in consequence of a stoppage of work due to a trade dispute; or

(b) an offer of employment in the district where he was last ordinarily employed at a rate of wage lower, or on conditions less favourable, than those which he habitually obtained in his usual employment in that district, or would have obtained had he continued to be so employed; or

(c) an offer of employment in any other district at a rate of wage lower or on conditions less favourable than those generally observed in such district by agreement between associations o employers and of workmen, or, failing any such agreement, than those generally recognised in such district by good employers.

87. (1) A workman who has lost employment by reason of a stoppage of work which was due to a trade dispute at the factory, workshop, or other premises at which he was employed, shall be disqualified for receiving unemployment benefit so long as the stoppage of work continues, except in a case where he has, during the stoppage of work, become bona fide employed elsewhere in an insured trade.

Where separate branches of work which are commonly carried on as separate businesses in separate premises are in any case carried on in separate departments on the same premises, each of those departments shall, for the purposes of this provision, be deemed to be a separate factory or workshop or separate premises, as the case may be.

(2) A workman who loses employment through misconduct or who voluntarily leaves his employment without just cause shall be disqualified from receiving unemployment benefit for a period of six weeks from the date when he so lost employment.

(3) A workman shall be disqualified from receiving unemployment benefit whilst he is an inmate of any prison or any workhouse or other institution supported wholly or partly out of public funds, and whilst he is resident temporarily or permanently outside the United Kingdom.

(4) A workman shall be disqualified from receiving unemployment benefit while he is in receipt of any sickness or disablement benefit or disablement allowance under Part I, of this Act ... .

Sixth Schedule

List of insured trades for the purposes of Part II of this Act relating to unemployment insurance

(1) Building; that is to say, the construction, alteration, repair, decoration, or demolition of buildings, including the manufacture of any fittings or wood of a kind commonly made in builders' workshops or yards.

(2) Construction of works; that is to say, the construction, reconstruction, or alteration of railroads, docks, harbours, canals, embankments, bridges, piers or other works of construction.

(3) Shipbuilding; that is to say, the construction, alteration, repair or decoration of ships, boats or other craft by persons not being usually members of a ship's crew, including the manufacture of any fittings of wood of a kind commonly made in a shipbuilding yard.

(4) Mechanical engineering, including the manufacture of ordnance and firearms.

(5) Ironfounding, whether included under the foregoing headings or not.

(6) Construction of vehicles; that is to say, the construction, repair, or decoration of vehicles.

(7) Sawmilling (including machine woodwork) carried on in connection with any other insured trade or of a kind commonly so carried on.

Seventh Schedule

Rates and periods of unemployment benefit

In respect of each week following the first week of any period of unemployment, seven shillings, or such other rates as may be prescribed either generally or for any particular trade or any branch thereof:

Provided that, in the case of a workman under the age of eighteen, no unemployment benefit shall be paid while the workman is below the age of seventeen, and while the workman is of the age of seventeen or upwards but below the age of eighteen, unemployment benefit shall only be paid at half the rate at which it would be payable if the workman was above the age of eighteen.

No workman shall receive unemployment benefit for more than fifteen or such other number of weeks as may be prescribed either generally or for any particular trade or branch thereof within any period of twelve months, or in respect of any period less than one day.

No workman shall receive more unemployment benefit than in the proportion of one week's benefit for every five contributions paid by him under this Act:

Provided that for the purpose of the foregoing paragraph:

(a) in the case of a workman who satisfies the Board of Trade that he is over the age of twenty-one and has habitually worked at an insured trade before the commencement of this Act, there shall be deemed to be added to the number of contributions which he has actually paid five contributions for each period of three months or part of such period during which he has so worked before the commencement of this Act, up to a maximum of twenty-five contributions; and

(b) where, owing to the fact that the wages or other remuneration of a workman are paid at intervals greater than a week, or for any other like reason contributions are paid under Part II of this Act in respect of any workman at intervals greater than a week, that workman shall be entitled to treat each of such contributions as so many contributions as there are weeks in the period for which the contribution has been paid. Any time during which a workman is, under Part II of this Act, disqualified for receiving unemployment benefit shall be excluded in the computation of periods of unemployment under this schedule.

A period of unemployment shall not be deemed to commence till the workman has made application for unemployment benefit in such manner as may be prescribed.

The power conferred by this schedule on the Board of Trade to prescribe rates and periods of unemployment benefit shall not be exercised so as to increase the rate of benefit above eight shillings per week or reduce it below six shillings per week, or to increase the period of unemployment benefit above fifteen weeks, or to alter the proportion which the period of benefit bears to the number of contributions paid, except by rules confirmed by an order made in accordance with the provisions of this Act relating to special orders.

Eighth Schedule

Contributions for the purposes of Part II of this Act relating to unemployment insurance

Rates of contribution from workmen and employers.

From every workman employed in an insured trade for every week he is so employed .... 2½*d.*

From every employer by whom one or more workmen are employed in an insured trade, in respect of each workman, for every week he is so employed .... 2½*d.*

Provided that, in the case of a workman below the age of eighteen, 1*d.* shall be substituted for 2½*d.* as the contribution from the workman and from the employer, but, for the purpose of reckoning the number of contributions in respect of such a workman except as regards the payment of unemployment benefit before he reaches the age of eighteen, the 1*d.* shall be treated as two-fifths of a contribution. Every such period of employment of less than a week shall, for the purposes of this schedule, be treated as if it were employment for a whole week, except that, where the period of employment is two days or less, the contributions both of the employer and of the workman shall be reduced to one penny if the period does not exceed one day and to twopence if it exceeds one day; and, in such case, in reckoning the number of contributions under Part II of this Act and the schedules therein referred to, contributions at such reduced rates shall be treated as two-fifths of a contribution as the case may require.

(National Insurance Act, London, 1911)

I.13 From the Treaty of Versailles (1919)

Article 88

Annex

1.

Within fifteen days from the coming into force of the present Treaty the German troops and such officials as may be designated by the Commission set up under the provisions of paragraph 2 shall evacuate the plebiscite area. Up to the moment of the completion of the evacuation they shall refrain from any form of requisitioning in money or in kind and from all acts likely to prejudice the material interests of the country.

Within the same period the Workmens' and Soldiers' Councils which have been constituted in this area shall be dissolved. Members of such Councils who are natives of another region and are exercising their functions at the date of the coming into force of the present Treaty, or who have gone out of office since March 1, 1919, shall be evacuated.

All military and semi-military unions formed in the said area by inhabitants of the district shall be immediately disbanded. All members of such military organizations who are not domiciled in the said area shall be required to leave it.

2.

The plebiscite area shall be immediately placed under the authority of an International Commission of four members to be designated by the following Powers; the United States of America, France, the British Empire and Italy. It shall be occupied by troops belonging to the Allied and Associated Powers, and the German Government undertakes to give facilities for the transference of these troops to Upper Silesia.

3.

The Commission shall enjoy all the powers exercised by the German or the Prussian Government, except those of legislation or taxation. It shall also be substituted for the government of the province and the *Regierungsbezirk.*

It shall be within the competence of the Commission to interpret the powers hereby conferred upon it and to determine to what extent it shall exercise them, and to what extent they shall be left in the hands of the existing authorities.

Changes in the existing laws and the existing taxation shall only be brought into force with the consent of the Commission.

The Commission will maintain order with the help of the troops which will be at its disposal, and, to the extent which it may deem necessary, by means of gendarmerie recruited among the inhabitants of the country.

The Commission shall provide immediately for the replacement of the evacuated German officials and, if occasion arises, shall itself order the evacuation of such authorities and proceed to the replacement of such local authorities as may be required.

It shall take all steps which it thinks proper to ensure the freedom, fairness and secrecy of the vote. In particular, it shall have the right to order the expulsion of any person who may in any way have attempted to distort the result of the plebiscite by methods of corruption or intimidation.

The Commission shall have full power to settle all questions arising from the execution of the present clauses. It shall be assisted by technical advisers chosen by it from among the local population.

The decisions of the Commission shall be taken by a majority vote.

4.

The vote shall take place at such date as may be determined by the Principal Allied and Associated Powers, but not sooner than six months or later than eighteen months after the establishment of the Commission in the area. The right to vote shall be given to all persons without distinction of sex who:

(a) Have completed their twentieth year on the lst January of the year in which the plebiscite takes place;

(b) Were born in the plebiscite area or have been domiciled there since a date to be determined by the Commission, which shall not be subsequent to the 1st

January, 1919, or who have been expelled by the German authorities and have not retained their domicile there.

Persons convicted of political offences shall be enabled to exercise their right of voting.

Every person will vote in the commune where he is domiciled or in which he was born, if he has not retained his domicile in the area.

The result of the vote will be determined by communes according to the majority of votes in each commune.

5.

On the conclusion of the voting, the number of votes cast in each commune will be communicated by the Commission to the Principal Allied and Associated Powers, with a full report as to the taking of the vote and a recommendation as to the line which ought to be adopted as the frontier of Germany in Upper Silesia. In this recommendation regard will be paid to the wishes of the inhabitants as shown by the vote, and to the geographical and economic conditions of the locality.

6.

As soon as the frontier has been fixed by the Principal Allied and Associated Powers, the German authorities will be notified by the International Commission that they are free to take over the administration of the territory which it is recognised should be German; the said authorities must proceed to do so within one month of such notification and in the manner prescribed by the Commission.

Within the same period and in the manner prescribed by the Commission, the Polish Government must proceed to take over the administration of the territory which it is recognised should be Polish.

When the administration of the territory has been provided for by the German and Polish authorities respectively, the powers of the Commission will terminate.

The cost of the army of occupation, and expenditure by the Commission, whether in discharge of its own functions or in the administration of the territory, will be a charge on the area ... .

Article 91

German nationals habitually resident in territories recognized as forming part of Poland will acquire Polish nationality *ipso facto* and will lose their German nationality.

German nationals, however, or their descendants who became resident in these territories after January 1, 1908, will not acquire Polish nationality without a special authorization from the Polish State.

Within a period of two years after the coming into force of the present Treaty, German nationals over 18 years of age habitually resident in any of the territories recognized as forming part of Poland will be entitled to opt for German nationality.

Poles who are German nationals over 18 years of age and habitually resident in Germany will have a similar right to opt for Polish nationality.

Option by a husband will cover his wife and option by parents will cover their children under 18 years of age.

Persons who have exercised the above right to opt may within the succeeding twelve months transfer their place of residence to the State for which they have opted.

They will be entitled to retain their immovable property in the territory of the other State where they had their place of residence before exercising the right to opt.

They may carry with them their movable property of every description. No export or import duties or charges may be imposed upon them in connection with the removal of such property.

Within the same period Poles who are German nationals and are in a foreign country will be entitled, in the absence of any provisions to the contrary in the foreign law, and if they have not acquired the foreign nationality, to obtain Polish nationality and to lose their German nationality by complying with the requirements laid down by the Polish State.

In the portion of Upper Silesia submitted to a plebiscite the provisions of this Article shall only come into force as from the definitive attribution of the territory.

...

Article 92

The proportion and the nature of the financial liabilities of Germany and Prussia which are to be borne by Poland will be determined in accordance with Article 254 of Part IX (Financial Clauses) of the present Treaty.

There shall be excluded from the share of such financial liabilities assumed by Poland that portion of the debt which, according to the finding of the Reparation Commission referred to in the above-mentioned Article, arises from measures adopted by the German and Prussian Governments with a view to German colonization in Poland.

In fixing under Article 256 of the present Treaty the value of the property and possessions belonging to the German Empire and to the German States which pass to Poland with the territory transferred above, the Reparation Commission shall exclude from the valuation buildings, forests and other State property which belonged to the former Kingdom of Poland; Poland shall acquire these properties free of all costs and charges.

In all the German territory transferred in accordance with the present Treaty and recognized as forming definitively part of Poland, the property, rights and interests of German nationals shall not be liquidated under Article 297 by the Polish Government except in accordance with the following provisions:

1. The proceeds of the liquidation shall be paid direct to the owner;
2. If on his application the Mixed Arbitral Tribunal provided for by Section VI of Part X (Economic Clauses) of the present Treaty, or an arbitrator appointed by that Tribunal, is satisfied that the conditions of the sale or measures taken by the Polish Government outside its general legislation were unfairly prejudicial to the price obtained, they shall have discretion to

award to the owner equitable compensation to be paid by the Polish Government.

Further agreements will regulate all questions arising out of the cession of the above territory which are not regulated by the present Treaty.

Article 93

Poland accepts and agrees to embody in a Treaty with the Principal Allied and Associated–'Powers such provisions as may be deemed necessary by the said Powers to protect the interests of inhabitants of Poland who differ from the majority of the population in race, language or religion.

Poland further accepts and agrees to embody in a Treaty with the said Powers such provisions as they may deem necessary to protect freedom of transit and equitable treatment of the commerce of other nations.

...

Penalties

Article 227

The Allied and Associated Powers publicly arraign William II of Hohenzollern, formerly German Emperor, for a supreme offence against international morality and the sanctity of treaties.

A special tribunal will be constituted to try the accused, thereby assuring him the guarantees essential to the right of defence. It will be composed of five judges, one appointed by each of the following Powers: namely, the United States of America, Great Britain, France, Italy and Japan.

In its decision the tribunal will be guided by the highest motives of inetrnational policy, with a view to vindicating the solemn obligations of international undertakings and the validity of international morality. It will be its duty to fix the punishment which it considers should be imposed.

The Allied and Associated Powers will address a request to the Government of the Netherlands for the surrender to them of the ex-Emperor in order that he may be put on trial.

Article 228

The German Government recognises the right of the Allied and Associated Powers to bring before military tribunals persons accused of having committed acts in violation of the laws and customs of war. Such persons shall, if found guilty, be sentenced to punishments laid down by the law. This provision will apply notwithstanding any proceedings or prosecution before a tribunal in Germany or in the territory of her allies.

'War Guilt' and Reparations

Article 231

The Allied and Associated Governments affirm and Germany accepts the responsibility of Germany and her allies for causing all the loss and damage to which the Allied and Associated Governments and their nationals have been subjected as a consequence of the war imposed upon them by the aggression of Germany and her allies ... .

Article 232

The Allied and Associated Governments recognize that the resources of Germany are not adequate, after taking into account permanent diminutions of such resources which will result from other provisions of the present Treaty, to make complete reparation for all such loss and damage.

The Allied and Associated Governments, however, require, and Germany undertakes, that she will make compensation for all damage done to the civilian population of the Allied and Associated Powers and to their propety during the period of the belligerency of each as an Allied or Associated Power against Germany by such aggression by land, by sea and from the air, and in general all damage as defined in Annex I hereto.

In accordance with Germany's pledges, already given, as to complete restoration for Belgium, Germany undertakes, in addition to the compensation for damage elsewhere in this Part provided for, as a consequence of the violation of the Treaty of 1839, to make reimbursement of all sums which Belgium has borrowed from the Allied and Associated Governments up to November 11, 1918, together with interest at the rate of five per cent. (5%) per annum on such sums ...

Article 233

The amount of the above damage for which compensation is to be made by Germany shall be determined by an Inter-Allied Commission, to be called the *Reparation Commission* and constituted in the form and with the powers set forth hereunder and in Annexes II to VII inclusive hereto.

This Commission shall consider the claims and give to the German Government a just opportunity to be heard.

The findings of the Commission as to the amount of damage defined as above shall be concluded and notified to the German Government on or before May 1, 1921, as representing the extent of that Governments's obligations.

The Commission shall concurrently draw up a schedule of payments prescribing the time and manner for securing and discharging the entire obligation within a period of thirty years from May 1, 1921. If, however, within the period mentioned Germany fails to discharge her obligations, any balance remaining unpaid may, within the discretion of the Commission, be postponed for settlement in subsequent years , or may be handled otherwise in such manner as the Allied and Associated Governments, acting in accordance with the procedure laid down in this Part of the present Treaty, shall determine.

...

Article 387

A permanent organization is hereby established for the promotion of the objects set forth in the Preamble.

The original Members of the League of Nations shall be the original Members of this organization, and hereafter membership of the League of Nations shall carry with it membership of the said organization.

Article 388

The permanent organization shall consist of:

1. a General Conference of Representatives of the Members and,
2. an International Labour Office controlled by the Governing Body described in Article 393....

Article 390

Every Delegate shall be entitled to vote individually on all matters which are taken into consideration by the Conference.

If one of the Members fails to nominate one of the non-Government Delegates whom it is entitled to nominate, the other non-Government Delegate shall be allowed to sit and speak at the Conference, but not to vote

...

Article 427

The High Contracting Parties, recognizing that the well-being, physical, moral and intellectual, of industrial wage-earners is of supreme international importance, have framed, in order to further this great end, the permanent machinery provided for in Section 1 and associated with that of the League of Nations.

They recognize that differences of climate, habits and customs, of economic opportunity and industrial tradition, make strict uniformity in the conditions of labour difficult of immediate attainment. But, holding as they do, that labour should not be regarded merely as an article of commerce they think that there are methods and principles for regulating labour conditions which all industrial communities should endeavour to apply, so far as their special circumstances will permit.

Among these methods and principles, the following seem to the High Contracting Parties to be of special and urgent importance:

First. – The guiding principle above enunciated that labour should not be regarded merely as a commodity or article of commerce.

Second. – The right of association for all lawful purposes by the employed as well as by the employers.

Third. – The payment to the employed of a wage adequate to maintain a reasonable standard of life as this is understood in their time and country.

Fourth. – The adoption of an eight hours day or a forty-eight hours week as the standard to be aimed at where it has not already been attained.

Fifth. – The adoption of a weekly rest of at least twenty-four hours, which should include Sunday wherever practicable.

Sixth. – The abolition of child labour and the imposition of such limitations on the labour of young persons as shall permit the continuation of their education and assure their proper physical development.

Seventh. – The principle that men and women should receive equal remuneration for work of equal value.

Eighth. – The standard set by law in each country with respect to the conditions of labour should have due regard to the equitable economic treatment of all workers lawfully resident therein.

Ninth. – Each State should make provision for a system of inspection in which women should take part, in order to ensure the enforcement of the laws and regulations for the protection of the employed.

Without claiming that these methods and principles are either complete or final, the High Contracting Parties are of opinion that they are well fitted to guide the policy of the League of Nations; and that, if adopted by the industrial communities who are members of the League, and safeguarded in practice by an adequate system of such inspection, they will confer lasting benefits upon the wage-earners of the world.

(Papers Relating to the Foreign Relations of the United States. The Paris Peace Conference 1919, Volume XIII, Washington, 1947, pp.371–428)

I.14 Memorandum by Sir Eyre Crowe: 'The aims of German policy' (1907)

With the events of 1871 the spirit of Prussia passed into the new Germany. In no other country is there a conviction so deeply rooted in the very body and soul of all classes of the population that the preservation of national rights and the realization of national ideals rest absolutely on the readiness of every citizen in the last resort to stake himself and his State on their assertion and vindication. With 'blood and iron' Prussia had forged her position in the councils of the great powers of Europe. In due course it came to pass that, with the impetus given to every branch of national activity by the newly won unity and more especially by the growing development of overseas trade flowing in ever-increasing volume through the now imperial ports of the formerly 'independent' but politically insignificant Hanse towns, the young empire found opened to its energy a whole world outside Europe, of which it had previously hardly had the opportunity to become more than dimly conscious. Sailing across the ocean in German ships, German merchants began for the first time to divine the true position of countries such as England, the United States, France and even the Netherlands, whose political influence extends to distant seas and continents. The colonies and foreign possessions of England more especially were seen to give to that country a recognized and enviable status in a world where the name of Germany, if mentioned at all, excited no particular interest. The effect of this discovery upon the German mind was curious and instructive. Here was a vast province of human activity to which the mere title and rank of a European great power were not in themselves a sufficient passport. Here in a field of portentous magnitude, dwarfing altogether the proportions of European countries, others, who had been perhaps rather looked down upon as comparatively smaller folk, were at home and commanded, while Germany was at best received but as an honoured guest. Here was distinct inequality, with a heavy bias in favour of the maritime and colonizing powers.

Such a state of things was not welcome to German patriotic pride. Germany had won her place as one of the leading, if not, in fact, the foremost power on the European continent. But over and beyond the European great powers there seemed to stand the 'world powers'. It was at once clear that Germany must become a 'world power'. The evolution of this idea and its translation into practical politics followed with singular consistency the line of thought that had inspired the Prussian kings in their efforts to make Prussin great. 'If Prussia', said Frederick the Great, 'is to count for something in the councils of Europe, she must be made a great power.' And the echo: 'If Germany wants to have a voice in the affairs of the larger oceanic world she must be made a "world power".' 'I want more territory,' said Prussia. 'Germany must have colonies,' says the new world-policy. And colonies were accordingly established, in such spots as were found to be still unappropriated, or out of which others could be pushed by the vigorous assertion of a German demand for 'a place in the sun'. On the whole, however, the 'Colonies' have proved assets of somewhat doubtful value.

Meanwhile the dream of a colonial empire had taken deep hold on the German imagination. Emperor, statesmen, journalists, geographers, economists, commercial and shipping houses and the whole mass of educated and uneducated public opinion continue with one voice to declare: We *must* have real colonies, where German emigrants can settle and spread the national ideals of the Fatherland and we *must* have a fleet and coaling stations to keep together the colonies which we are bound to acquire ... .

No one who has a knowledge of German political thought and who enjoys the confidence of German friends speaking their minds openly and freely, can deny that these are the ideas which are proclaimed on the housetops and that inability to sympathize with them is regarded in Germany as the mark of the prejudiced foreigner who cannot enter into the real feelings of Germans. Nor is it amiss to refer in this connection to the series of Imperial apophthegms, which have from time to time served to crystallize the prevailing German sentiments and some of which deserve quotation: 'Our future lies on the water.' 'The trident must be in our hand.' 'Germany must re-enter into her heritage of maritime dominion once unchallenged in the hands of the old Hansa.' 'No question of world politics must be settled without the consent of the German Emperor.' 'The Emperor of the Atlantic greets the Emperor of the Pacific,' etc.

The significance of these individual utterances may easily be exaggerated. Taken together, their cumulative effect is to confirm the impression that Germany distinctly aims at playing on the world's political stage a much larger and much more dominant part than she finds allotted to herself under the present distribution of material power ... .

If it be considered necessary to formulate and accept a theory that will fit all the ascertained facts of German foreign policy the choice must lie between the two hypotheses here presented:

Either Germany is definitely aiming at a general political hegemony and maritime ascendency, threatening the independence of her neighbours and ultimately the existence of England;

Or Germany, free from any such clear-cut ambition and thinking for the present merely of using her legitimate position and influence as one of the leading powers in the council of nations, is seeking to promote her foreign commerce, spread the benefits of German culture, extend the scope of her national energies and create fresh German interests all over the world wherever and whenever a peaceful opportunity offers, leaving it to an uncertain future to decide whether the occurrence of great changes in the world may not some day assign to Germany a larger share of direct political action over regions not now a part of her dominions without that violation of the established rights of other countries which would be involved in any such action under existing political conditions.

In either case Germany would clearly be wise to build as powerful a navy as she can afford.

The above alternatives seem to exhaust the possibilities of explaining the given facts. The choice offered is a narrow one, nor easy to make with any close approach to certainty. It will, however, be seen, on reflection, that there is no actual necessity for a British Government to determine definitely which of the two theories of German policy it will accept. For it is clear that the second scheme (of semi-independent evolution, not entirely unaided by statecraft) may at any stage merge into the first, or conscious-design scheme. Moreover, if ever the evolution scheme should come to be realized, the position thereby accruing to Germany would obviously constitute as formidable a menace to the rest of the world as would be presented by any deliberate conquest of a similar position by 'malice aforethought'.

It appears, then, that the element of danger present as a visible factor in one case, also enters, though under some disguise, into the second; and against such danger, whether actual or contingent, the same general line of conduct seems prescribed.

(G.P. Gooch and H. Temperley, *British Documents on the Origins of the War*, Vol. III, Appendix A. H.M.S.O., from John Röhl (ed.) *From Bismarck to Hitler*, p.60/63)

I.15 Admiral von Müller's (Chief of the Imperial Naval Cabinet) diary entry (8 Dec. 1912)

Sunday, Ordered to see His Maj. at the Schloss at 11 a.m. with Tirpitz, Heeringen (vice Admiral) and General von Moltke. H.M. speaks to a telegraphic report from the Ambassador in London, Prince Lichnowsky, concerning the political situation. Haldane, speaking for Grey, has told Lichnowsky that England, if we attacked France, would unconditionally spring to France's aid, for England could not allow the balance of power in Europe to be disturbed. H.M. greeted this information as a desirable clarification of the situation for the benefit of those who had felt sure of England as a result of the recent friendliness of the press.

H.M. envisaged the following:

Austria must deal energetically with the foreign Slavs (the Serbs), otherwise she will lose control of the Slavs in the Austro-Hungarian monarchy. If Russia supports the Serbs, which she evidently does (Sasonoff's declaration that Russia will immediately move into Galicia if Austria moves into Serbia) then war would be unavoidable for us too. We could hope, however, to have Bulgaria and Rumania and also Albania, and perhaps also Turkey on our side. An offer of alliance by Bulgaria has already been sent to Turkey. We have exerted great pressure on the Turks. Recently H.M. has also pressed the Crown Prince of Rumania, who was passing through on his way back from Brussels, to come to an understanding with Bulgaria. If these powers join Austria then we shall be free to fight the war with full fury against France. The fleet must naturally prepare itself for the war against England. The possibility mentioned by the Chief of the Admiralty Staff in his last audience of a war with Russia alone cannot now, after Haldane's statement, be taken into account. Therefore immediate submarine warfare against English troop transports in the Scheldt or by Dunkirk, mine warfare in the Thames. To Tirpitz [the state secretary]: speedy build-up of U-boats, etc. Recommendation of a conference of all naval authorities concerned.

General von Moltke: 'I believe a war is unavoidable and the sooner the better. But we ought to do more through the press to prepare the popularity of a war against Russia, as suggested in the Kaiser's discussion.'

H.M. supported this and told the State Secretary [Tirpitz] to use his press contacts, too, to work in this direction. T[irpitz] made the observation that the navy would prefer to postpone the great fight for one and a half years. Moltke says the navy would not be ready even then and the army would get into an increasingly unfavourable position, for the enemies were arming more strongly than we, as we were very short of money.

This was the end of the conference. The result amounted to almost 0.

The Chief of the General Staff says: War the sooner the better, but he does not draw the logical conclusion from this, which is to present Russia or France or both with an ultimatum which would unleash the war with right on our side.

In the afternoon I wrote to the Reich Chancellor about the influencing of the press.

(from J. C. G. Röhl, *The Kaiser and his Court: Wilhelm II and the Government of Germany*, Cambridge 1994, pp.162/3)

I.16 Count Szögyény (Austro-Hungarian Ambassador to Berlin) to Count Berchtold (Austro-Hungarian Foreign Minister) (5 July 1914)

Berlin 5 July 1914 tel.237 Strictly Confidential

... The Kaiser authorised me to inform our Gracious Majesty that we might in this case, as in all others, rely upon Germany's full support ... . He did not doubt in the least that Herr von Bethmann Hollweg would agree with him. Especially as far as our action against Serbia was concerned. But it was his [Kaiser Wilhelm's] opinion that this action must not be delayed. Russia's attitude will no doubt be hostile, but for this he had for years prepared, and should a war between Austria-Hungary and Russia be unavoidable, we might be convinced that Germany, our old faithful ally, would stand on our side. Russia at the present time was in no way prepared for war, and would think twice before it appealed to arms ... . If we had really recognised the necessity of warlike action against Serbia, he [Kaiser Wilhelm] would regret if we did not make use of the present moment, which is all in our favour ... .

(From Imanuel Geiss (ed.) *July 1914. The Outbreak of the First World War: Selected Documents*, Batsford, 1967, pp.77)

I.17 Telegram from Sir Edward Grey (British Foreign Secretary) to Sir Edward Goschen (British Ambassador in Berlin) (31 July 1914)

London, 31 July 1914
D. 2.45 p.m.

European crisis. My telegram 413 of 31 July to St Petersberg, which has been repeated to you today.

I hope that the conversations which are now proceeding between Austria and Russia may lead to a satisfactory result. The stumbling-block hitherto has been Austrian mistrust of Serbian assurances, and Russian mistrust of Austrian intentions with regard to the independence and integrity of Serbia. It has occurred to me that in the event of this mistrust preventing a solution being found by Vienna and St Petersburg, Germany might sound Vienna, and I would undertake to sound St Petersburg, whether it would be possible for the four disinterested Powers to offer to Austria that they would undertake to see that she obtained full satisfaction of her demands on Serbia, provided that they did not impair Serbian sovereignty and the integrity of Serbian territory. As Your Excellency is aware, Austria has already declared her willingness to respect them.[1] Russia might be informed by the four Powers that they would undertake to prevent Austrian demands going the length of impairing Serbian sovereignty and integrity. All Powers would of course suspend further military operations or preparations.

You may sound the Secretary of State for Foreign Affairs[2] about this proposal.

I said to German Ambassador this morning that if Germany could get any reasonable proposal put forward which made it clear that Germany and Austria were striving to preserve European peace, and that Russia and France would be unreasonable if they rejected it, I would support it at St Petersburg and Paris and go the length of saying that if Russia and France would not accept it His Majesty's Government would have nothing more to do with the consequences; but, otherwise, I told German Ambassador that if France became involved we should be drawn in.

[1] This declaration, however, only applied to Serbia's territorial integrity.

[2] Gothlieb von ~~Jagow~~ Jagow

You can add this when sounding Chancellor[3] or Minister for Foreign Affairs as to proposal above. If you think it desirable, you can also give Chancellor a memorandum of my telegram 231 of yesterday; I presume you have told him of it verbally.

(From Imanuel Geiss (ed.) *July 1914. The Outbreak of the First World War, Selected Documents*, Batsford, 1967, p.329)

I.18 Memorandum of Prince Karl Max Lichnowsky (1914)

When I arrived in London in November 1912 the First Balkan War had really already ended with the Allies' victory over Turkey, and the disposal of the Turkish heritage raised the spectre of a European war.

A few days after my arrival, Lord Haldane, a close friend of Sir E. Grey's, visited me to tell me roughly the following: England desired peace and friendship with us, and hoped with my help to strengthen our relations and to remove all misunderstandings. But he drew my attention to one important point from the first: *England could never permit the destruction or weakening of France.* This was a vital question for Great Britain. She had to support France, as we had to support Austria. The basis of any understanding with us must therefore be *an unquestionable policy of peace*, since England would be drawn through France into a European war. But England no more wished to attack us than to foster the French idea of revanche ... .

On our side *nothing*, absolutely *nothing*, was done to preserve peace, and when we *at last* decided to do what I had advocated from the first, it was too late. By then Russia, as a result of our harsh attitude and that of Count Berchtold, had lost all confidence and mobilised. The war party gained the upper hand.... Such a policy is comprehensible only if war was our aim, not otherwise. The influential people at the [Foreign] Office repeatedly told me that Russia would be 'ready' in 1916, and that we should not wait for that. Our relations with Russia had visibly deteriorated, so much is true. But instead of trying to improve them by replacing personnel and by showing greater discretion in supporting Austrian wishes, as well as consideration for Russian sensibilities in other matters, we took up arms. Who can prove that we would really have had to fight in 1916? To what end would Russia have attacked us? *England and France were absolutely peaceable and would have remained* so; they would never have supported a Russian attack.

But the crucial questions are not: Did Grey want war? Why did he not prevent it? What did he do or not do to prevent it? – but rather: Did we want war? Why did *we* not prevent it? What did *we* do or not do to prevent it?

(Quoted by J. Röhl, in *1914: Delusion or Design? The Testimony of Two German Diplomats*, St. Albans, Elek, 1973)

[3] Theobald von Bethmann-Hollweg

PART II

II.1 From Bethmann's Memorandum: 'Provisional notes on the direction of our policy on the conclusion of peace' (9 Sept. 1914)

The 'general aim of the war' was, for him, 'security for the German Reich in west and east for all imaginable time. For this purpose France must be so weakened as to make her revival as a great power impossible for all time. Russia must be thrust back as far as possible from Germany's eastern frontier and her domination over the non-Russian vassal peoples broken.'

1. *France.* The military to decide whether we should demand cession of Belfort and western slopes of the Vosges, razing of fortresses and cession of coastal strip from Dunkirk to Boulogne.

   The ore-field of Briey, which is necessary for the supply of ore for our industry, to be ceded in any case.

   Further, a war indemnity, to be paid in instalments; it must be high enough to prevent France from spending any considerable sums on armaments in the next 15–20 years.

   Furthermore: a commercial treaty which makes France economically dependent on Germany, secures the French market for our exports and makes it possible to exclude British commerce from France. This treaty must secure for us financial and industrial freedom of movement in France in such fashion that German enterprises can no longer receive different treatment from French.

2. *Belgium.* Liège and Verviers to be attached to Prussia, a frontier strip of the province of Luxemburg to Luxemburg.

   Question whether Antwerp, with a corridor to Liège, should also be annexed remains open.

   At any rate Belgium, even if allowed to continue to exist as a state, must be reduced to a vassal state, must allow us to occupy any militarily important ports, must place her coast at our disposal in military respects, must become economically a German province. Given such a solution, which offers the advantages of annexation without its inescapable domestic political disadvantages, French Flanders with Dunkirk, Calais and Boulogne, where most of the population is Flemish, can without danger be attached to this unaltered Belgium. The competent quarters will have to judge the military value of this position against England.

3. *Luxemburg.* Will become a German federal state and will receive a strip of the present Belgian province of Luxemburg and perhaps the corner of Longwy.

4. We must create a *central European economic association* through common customs treaties, to include France, Belgium, Holland, Denmark, Austria-Hungary, Poland, and perhaps Italy, Sweden and Norway. This association will not have any common constitutional supreme authority and all its members will be formally equal, but in practice will be under German

leadership and must stabilise Germany's economic dominance over Mitteleuropa.

5. *The question of colonial acquisitions*, where the first aim is the creation of a continuous Central African colonial empire, will be considered later, as will that of the aims to be realised *vis-à-vis* Russia.
6. A short provisional formula suitable for a possible preliminary peace to be found for a basis for the economic agreements to be concluded with France and Belgium.
7. *Holland.* It will have to be considered by what means and methods Holland can be brought into closer relationship with the German Empire.

   In view of the Dutch character, this closer relationship must leave them free of any feeling of compulsion, must alter nothing in the Dutch way of life, and must also subject them to no new military obligations. Holland, then, must be left independent in externals, but be made internally dependent on us. Possibly one might consider an offensive and defensive alliance, to cover the colonies; in any case a close customs association, perhaps the cession of Antwerp to Holland in return for the right to keep a German garrison in the fortress of Antwerp and at the mouth of the Scheldt.

II.2 From *'The Peace Proposal':* letter from Bethmann Hollweg to Mr Joseph Clark Grew, Chargé d'Affaires of the United States of America (12 Dec. 1916)

Mr Chargé d'Affaires:

The most formidable war known to history has been ravaging for two and a half years over a great part of the world. That catastrophe, that the bonds of a common civilization more than a thousand years old could not stop, strikes mankind in its most precious patrimony; it threatens to bury under its ruin the moral and physical progress on which Europe prided itself at the dawn of the twentieth century. In that strife Germany and her allies, Austria-Hungary, Bulgaria and Turkey, have given proof of their indestructible strength in winning considerable successes at war. Their unshakable lines resist ceaseless attacks of their enemies' arms. The recent diversion in the Balkans was speedily and victoriously thwarted. The latest events have demonstrated that a continuation of the war cannot break their resisting power. The general situation much rather justifies their hope of fresh successes. It was for the defense of their existence and freedom of their national development that the four allied powers were constrained to take up arms. The exploits of their armies have brought no change therein. Not for an instant have they swerved from the conviction that the respect of the rights of other nations is not in any degree incompatible with their own rights and legitimate interests. They do not seek to crush or annihilate their adversaries. Conscious of their military and economic strength and ready to carry on to the end, if they must, the struggle that is forced upon them, but animated at the same time by the desire to stem the flood of blood and to bring the horrors of war to an end, the four allied powers propose to enter even now into peace negotiations. They feel sure that the propositions which they would bring forward, and which would aim to assure the existence, honor and free development of their peoples, would be such as to serve as a basis for the restoration of a lasting peace.

If, notwithstanding this offer of peace and conciliation, the struggle should continue, the four allied powers are resolved to carry it on to a victorious end, while solemnly disclaiming any responsibility before mankind and history.

The Imperial Government has the honor to ask through your obliging medium the Government of the United States to be pleased to transmit the present communication to the Government of the French Republic, to the Royal Government of Great Britain, to the Imperial Government of Japan, to the Royal Government of Rumania, to the Imperial Government of Russia, and to the Royal Government of Serbia.

I take this opportunity to renew to you, Mr. Chargé d'Affaires, the assurance of my high consideration.

von Bethmann Hollweg

(from *Fall of the German Empire, 1914–1918*, Volume I, pp.398–399 (ed.) Ralph Haswell Lutz, with the permission of the publishers, Stanford University Press,

II.3 First talk with General Ludendorff (16 Feb. 1917)

I called on Excellency Ludendorff at 12.30 p.m. at the General Staff where Headquarters has been located for the past few days. Colonel von Bartenwerffer was present during the conversation.

After a very friendly reception I commented on the state of the war economy as it appears to me from numerous indications. I described the cause of the production crisis: the execution of the Hindenburg Programme[4] had not led to new basic attitudes and new principles. On the contrary it had been commenced before everything was fully thought through.[5] No one had borne in mind that a

[4] The Hindenburg Programme was set up by the third Supreme Command. The Programme was to help increase the manufacture of weapons and munitions. On the strength of this the War Office was founded, in October 1916, and Groener was appointed as head on 1 November. Among the departments subordinate to the War Office were the KRA and the Weapons and Munitions Procurement Office. Feldman, *Army, Industry and Labor*, pp.149–96; Hiller von Gaertringen (ed.), *Wilhelm Groener*, pp.328–73.

[5] The Hindenburg Programme foundered because the quotas of explosives to be produced for the spring of 1917 could not be met. This failure was due to the excessive demands of the Programme and lack of organization. Feldman, *Army, Industry and Labor*, pp.266–73. See also Feldman, 'The Political and Social Foundations of Germany's Economic Mobilization', pp.134–42. Baudis and Nussbaum, *Wirtschaft und Staat*, pp.283 ff.

country which is absolutely occupied with making supplies for the war is not ready to be launched into a gigantic construction programme. Industrialists had been chivvied into building a great number of new factories which are just begun or half-finished today. The fact that the raw materials absorbed by this building would also contribute to the volume of trade in commodities in circulation had not been taken into consideration. Transport conditions had been accepted as they were, with no thought for the increased quantity [of goods] in circulation and increased production. The Auxiliary Service Law [*Hilfsdienstgesetz*][6] had suffered similarly; it too had originated from a sound and feasible idea, but that had been transformed into a legislative monster, so that today 150,000 people would be needed to carry it out and so it has in practice become unworkable. One of the causes of disorganization lies in over-organization, in the way committees and advisory bodies are constantly expanding, in the way attention is continually paid to deputies, interested parties and parliaments, so that things have now reached the stage where directions and principles cannot be adhered to because of committee meetings, conferences, and the work of organization.

(from *Walther Rathenau, Industrialist, Banker, Intellectual, and Politician. Notes and Diaries 1907–1922* (ed.) Hartmut Pogge von Strandmann, trans. Caroline Pinder-Cracraft, Oxford, Clarendon Press 1985)

II.4 'Programme of the Union of Economic Interests' [a French employers' organization] (7 April 1919)

1. Defence of property and of private enterprise. Freedom of agriculture, commerce, industry and labour. Protection of commercial property.
2. Formal opposition to any creation of new monopolies, to any experiments in collectivist socialization, to all control by the State over any services of a commercial or industrial character, to the exploitation by the State of services presently in its hands, and in general to all interference by the State in the running of private undertakings.

   The end of State consortiums.

   More efficient organization of existing monopolies, the present management of which conflicts with the interests of the public and of the Treasury.
3. The obligation of the State to observe the contracts it has signed. An embargo on the introduction of new charges without the consent of those holding contracts and without prior agreement as to compensation.

   Reassertion of the principle forbidding retrospective legislation.

...

[6] The Auxiliary Service Law came into force on 5 December 1916. It did not fulfil the hopes expressed in the law, because the shortage of labour remained a problem. Feldman, *Army, Industry and Labor*, pp.301–48; Armeson, *Total Warfare and Compulsory Labor*, chs. 4, 7, and 8; Baudis and Nussbaum, *Wirtschaft und Staat*, pp.285–8.

6. ...Compulsory and enforceable consultation of mandated representatives from the legally constituted Chambers of Commerce, Professional Bodies, and Groups of Economic Interests in all projects and legislative proposals relating to the economic life in the country.
7. The union of Capital and Labour Co-operation among employers and industrial and white-collar workers. Resolution of matters of concern in a spirit of unity, liberty and peace.
8. Co-ordination of social welfare legislation taking account of the economic needs of different regions and employers.

   Effective application of the weekly day of rest.
9. Administrative reorganization and decentralization in face of the advance of national and regional initiatives.
10. Organization of technical education and apprenticeship in collaboration with interested professional organizations.
11. Assistance to large families.

    Action against depopulation and all of its causes: tuberculosis, slum housing, alcohol abuse, etc. Proper enforcement of all existing legislation aimed at the suppression of public drunkenness.
12. Adoption of a legislative decree forbidding withdrawal of labour in any public service, whether run by the State or by private concession.

(Georges Lefranc, *Les organisations patronales en France*, Paris, Payot, 1976, pp.328–9; trans. A. Marwick)

II.5 Memorandum of the Neukölln Municipal Council to the War Food Department (3 Dec. 1917)

The increasing disquiet among our population and particularly among workmen employed in munition factories induces us to draw attention to the conditions of food supply. Remedial measures are urgently necessary, for the existing state of food distribution is according to our conviction the primary cause of the prevailing discontent.

At Neukölln about 1,300 establishments are employed on war work. Of these about 350 employ more than 50 persons each. Six of them employ more than 1,000 persons each. Following the example of great industrial concerns (such as those of Krupp, the AEG, Borsig, etc.) the larger establishments at Neukölln have employed agents to purchase foodstuffs, which they sold to their workpeople in order to supplement the official rations. Generally, these purchasing agents paid more than the official maximum prices in order to secure the commodities. In reselling foodstuffs to their workpeople some of the firms distributed them at the maximum retail prices and had, therefore, to defray the difference from their own funds. Other firms sold the goods at cost price and thereby violated the order fixing maximum prices. The result of this practice in the large munition works has been that the owners of small concerns engaged on war contracts have presented demands to the communal authorities that similar advantages in the procuring of food supplies should be secured for their employees also. These firms declare their inability to effect purchases; for, as a rule, the question of delivery by trucks is involved, and these vehicles are not so accessible to them as they are to the large firms, the latter being usually backed up by the Central Purchase Company and by government departments. The military inspecting officers support the petition of the smaller firms; and in order to obviate causes of unrest among the workpeople, the Town Council has felt compelled to purchase foodstuffs in the open market so as to place them at the disposal of these firms for distribution. In these cases, also, it has become necessary to exceed the maximum prices. The supplies obtained by the Town Council consisted, for the most part, of imported goods. To enable the Town Council to procure supplies by legal means, application was repeatedly made for import permits; but these were refused. By means of the measures adopted by the Town Council, on the recommendation of the local organizations, it was found possible to raise the workers employed at small shops to an approximate equality with those employed in the large establishments. Though the Town Council did not succeed in giving perfect satisfaction – for some inequality persists – it is able to claim at least that it has allayed the general discontent among workpeople. Until the beginning of October, therefore, conditions were fairly satisfactory. Since that time, much discontent has been manifested, because the large establishments, recognizing the increasing scarcity of food, have got hold of all the stocks within their reach. Many urban authorities have followed this example, and those communes which have striven to observe the provisions of the pertinent decrees (at least in matters of primary importance) find themselves confronted with an insoluble problem as regards their future supply of food. To this position we have been brought in consequence of the complete collapse of the economic system of the government departments. This assertion we proceed to demonstrate in regard to various foodstuffs in the paragraphs which follow:

(a) Corn and flour supply. The system for supplying corn or flour, it must be recognized, has been founded on a solid basis, so far as consignments to the communal unions are concerned. The only loophole in the organization is the arrangement for dealing with the seed corn of individual farms. These exceptional arrangements conduce to the result that very large quantities of grain still find their way into unregulated commerce. From aggressive merchants the council receives, in large numbers, offers of seed-corn licenses. Some of these offers are for quantities as large as 3,000 metric centners, or even more. For wheat, oats, and barley, the price asked is as much as 200 marks. the recognized trade price being only 100 marks. These offers are by no means fictitious; on the contrary, if contracts were concluded, deliveries would be well assured.

(b) Leguminous produce. Seed peas, beans, horse beans, and vetches are offered to the council at prices ranging between 140 and 260 marks per centner, no seed licences being annexed. As the price of 240 marks asked by one merchant seemed to the council to be too high, we declined the offer; and then another of the Greater Berlin Municipal Authorities accepted it. The quantity, in this case, was 3,100 centners, and the occasion of extortion complaints was the arrangement in regard to seed ... .

The maximum price fixed for beet is 1.75 marks; but to this nobody pays any heed. The market price at which beet is quite openly bought and sold may be quoted. A few weeks ago this market price for beet was 3.60 marks; and subsequently it has advanced to 4.75 or even 5 marks. The maximum price of horse beans being 30 marks, the smugglers' price is 110 marks a centner. The maximum price of vetches being 28 marks; supplies are offered at 100 and 105 marks.

This panorama is on exhibition in every borough and in every industrial district, more or less prominently. Competition exists between industrial concerns and those towns in which no food is produced, and this competition is recklessly exploited by extortioners. The latter find their advantage in the fact that those with whom they do business, while conscious of the illegality of their procedure, conspire to keep silence. Hence the extortioners can always allege, without fear of contradiction, that such and such a town council has already paid so much in excess of the maximum price. Should anybody take the trouble to find out the exact truth he will get no trustworthy information. Furthermore, the representatives of communal authorities will persist in the denial of facts unless and until they can be confronted with indisputable evidence. At a meeting of the Distribution Board of Greater Berlin, held before the president in the office of the Vegetable Control Board, it was ascertained, after a long debate, that every communal authority represented at the meeting had exceeded the maximum prices in purchasing vegetables. Charlottenburg claimed commendation because in purchasing supplies from producers it had not exceeded the prices payable to wholesale dealers. Town Councils which do not commit these illegalities run the risk that their burgesses will be worse off in regard to food supplies than those of towns where the councils betake themselves to forbidden paths.

The Town Council is convinced that it has, by the foregoing statements, shown the necessity for the application of amendments to the food supply system; that in particular the system of concluding contracts with producers is entirely ineffective for insuring an equitable distribution of foodstuffs; and that smuggling can be suppressed only by subjecting all foodstuffs to official embargo, so that no foodstuffs shall be subject to a mixed system of regulated and unregulated trade. The mixed system simply prepares the way for extortion, since unrestricted dealers pounce on the foodstuffs not subject to embargo and drive prices upward, the consequence being that commodities find their way to the places where most money can be obtained.

Shortage and famine (as ancient experience proves, and as the war has demonstrated afresh) may be endured with comparative ease when brought about by sheer necessity and when the victims are convinced that their fellow-mortals are subject to the same calamity. But resentment is aroused when the facts of the case are otherwise. Hence an equitable distribution of existing foodstuffs is imperatively necessary at the present time. That this end can be attained merely by the issue of orders and the threat of penalties seems in view of actual experience to be a highly doubtful proposition, since the authorities themselves find it necessary to ignore their own orders so as to effect some improvement in the distribution of supplies – such an improvement being unattainable through legal methods. The Town Council is of opinion that an advantageous rearrangement can result only from a general seizure of all foodstuffs in the localities where they are produced. This seizure should not be executed merely by the agency of interested persons – such persons as generally compose the war companies – but by impartial vigilance committees. For this reason the Town Council brings forward the following proposals for alleviating popular discontent:

(a) Places where foodstuffs are produced, associations of dealers, the homes of producers, distribution boards, etc., should be placed under the supervision of a Vigilance Committee, consisting of six members, of whom at least four should belong to consumers' districts. So far as the delivery of field products is concerned, the consumers' representatives should consist of persons selected from the districts of the organizations requiring commodities. For all matters concerning industrial products, the consumers' representatives should be selected from the trade unions of the branch of industry concerned. The Vigilance Committee in the rural districts from which foodstuffs are obtained should act as an advisory and controlling body for the District Commissioner, while in the industrial districts it should act in a similar capacity for the head of the competent distribution board or war company. The decisions of the Vigilance Committee should be obligatory on the heads of boards controlling producers, dealers, and distributors, subject to any statutory right of objection appertaining to them. All objections to the decisions of the Vigilance Committee should be decided finally by the War Food Department.

(b) All foodstuffs should be commandeered and then transferred to demand offices for warehousing and distribution. Stocks of seeds should be safeguarded by the Vigilance Committee and distributed in accordance with the needs of cultivators.

(c) In large residential and industrial districts foodstuffs should be distributed in uniform quantities and according to a uniform system. For this purpose uniform food distribution boards should be set up for these districts, and particularly for residential and industrial districts that are closely interdependent.

The Town Council expects that in view of the present intolerable state of things – one that must inevitably precipitate a catastrophe – the War Food Department will adopt suitable measures, at the earliest possible moment, to insure the alleviation of the causes of discontent. The urban authorities of Neukölln by unanimous resolution have declared that they regard it as a primary duty to see that a supply of food shall without fail be within the reach of their population. They have declared further that in order to insure this they are disposed to pursue the illegal methods already adopted unless the War Food Department immediately provides a remedy, and indeed even if the economic ruin of the borough should be brought about by the payment of extortionate prices which the council will not be able to transfer to the shoulders of the poorer section of the burgesses.

The council asks for an opportunity of sending a deputation consisting of six members to discuss orally the prevalent state of distress.

THE ADMINISTRATIVE BOARD
THE MUNICIPAL COUNCIL

(R. L. Lutz, *Fall of the German Empire, 1914–18*, Palo Alto, Stanford University Press, 1932, pp.177–8, 184–6)

II.6 From the Care of Mothers and Young Children Act (London, 1915)

An Act to extend the Notification of Births Act, 1907, to Areas in which it has not been adopted, and to make further provisions in connection therewith for the Care of Mothers and Young Children.

2 (1) Any local authority within the meaning of the principal Act ... may, for the purpose of the care of expectant mothers, nursing mothers, and young children, exercise any powers which a sanitary authority has in the Public Health Acts, 1875 to 1907, or the Public Health (London) Act, 1891, as the case requires.

(2) Any expenses incurred in the exercise of these powers shall be defrayed in the same manner as expenses of the local authority are defrayed in the principal Act.

Any such powers may be exercised in such manner as the authority directs by a committee or committees which shall include women and may comprise, if it is thought fit, persons who are not members of the authority. Any such committee may be empowered by the authority by which it is appointed to incur expenses up to a limit for the time being fixed by the authority, and, if so empowered, shall report any expenditure by them to the authority in such manner and at such times as the authority may direct ... .

(Care of Mothers and Young Children Act, London, 29 July 1915)

II.7 Report of a schoolmaster from Mazerolles, Charente (1915–16)

During the first year everything went more or less well: mobilization had left us with enough men, and the harvesting and ploughing were done everywhere in time. But by the second year there were already some properties without farmers, and at the beginning of the third year, there were four abandoned properties in this commune. This is obviously disappointing, but if we recall that the younger classes, the last of the reservists, the auxiliaries declared unfit for active service, etc., had been called up by this time, so that the only hands left were old men, the situation may be said to be as good as human effort could hope to make it, the more so as agricultural machinery cannot be used in our hilly country. On those farms which have not been abandoned all the fields have been ploughed and sown, but they have not been dressed properly. The women and children have done the best they could. Those men who have not been called up never grudged their help. It is also true to say that agricultural exemptions, granted largely to the auxiliaries and as a last resort to reservists at the front, proved invaluable: soldiers on leave did the ploughing and the reaping, work impossible for women. Agricultural labourers are very scarce, and the cost of manpower reflects this fact: up to 8 and 10 francs per day for reaping. Complete hostility towards the use of German prisoners of war.

(J-J Becker, *The Great War and the French People*, Leamington Spa, Berg, 1985, pp.126–7)

II.8 Department of Charente: the cost of living (price changes in basic commodities, in francs) (15 Feb. 1920)

	1914	*1915*	*1916*	*1917*	*1918*	*1919*	*1920*
Bread (per 1/2 kg)	0.15	0.15	0.20	0.25	0.25	0.30	0.50
Meat: beef, veal, mutton, (good cuts)	1.25	1.25	1.50	2	4	5	5
Wine (per 100 litres)	20	60	80	100	110	125	125
Sugar (per 1/2 kg)	0.80	0.80	0.90	0.95	1.15	1.25	1.25
Cheese (Gruyère, Roquefort) (per ½ kg)	1.50	1.50	5	6	7	7	7
Butter (per 1/2 kg)	1.60	1.75	–	–	–	8	8
Eggs (per dozen)	1	1.20	3	5	6	8	6
Milk (per litre)	0.10	0.10	0.15	0.30	0.40	0.60	0.75
Coffee (per 1/2 kg)	5	3	3.50	4	4.50	5	5
Dried beans (standard)	0.25	0.25	0.40	0.60	0.75	1.50	1.50
Split peas (per 1/2 kg)	0.50	–	–	–	3	3.25	3.25
Lentils (per 1/2 kg)	0.40	–	–	–	–	2.90	2.90
Chickens (per 1/2 kg)	1.25	1.50	2	3	4	4.50	4.50
Paraffin (per litre)	0.40	0.55	0.65	1	1.10	0.90	0.80
Petrol (per litre)	0.30	0.80	1	1.40	1.50	1.40	1.40
Coal (per tonne)	55	60	70	115	130	110	140
Charcoal (per 10 kg)	7	10	25	30	40	35	35
A suit	70	200	250	300	325	400	400
A pair of shoes (men's)	20	35	40	45	50	80	80
Chalk (per box)	0.75	–	–	–	1.75	2	2
Steel nibs (per box)	1.30	3	3.75	4	5.50	7	7
Schoolbooks	1	1.25	1.50	1.75	2	2	2
Potatoes	0.05	0.05	0.10	0.30	0.40	0.25	0.25
An ordinary workhorse	800	–	–	–	–	3,000 to 4,000	–
A milch cow	200	–	–	–	–	1,500 to 1,800	–
A pair of working oxen	1,200	–	–	–	–	6,000 to 7,000	–
A fat pig	120	–	–	–	–	800	–
A sucking pig	30	–	–	–	–	150	–

(J-J. Becker, The Great War and the French People, Leamington Spa, Berg, 1985, p.128)

II.9 Dragolioub Yovanovitch, from *The Economic and Social Effects of the War in Serbia (1929)*

During the war, the peasants enlarged their horizons. Their needs developed. The women in particular changed greatly. More and more they abandoned national costume. The men too showed a certain tendency in this direction, but to a lesser extent than the women. They tended simply to adopt one element or another of European costume: a hat, waistcoat or even shoes, or even all three, but they did not generally go very far, or else they changed by stages. The women were more radical, particularly the young ones. Nowadays there are villages where on fete days one cannot find a single young peasant girl or young peasant woman in national costume. In the course of their movements from one place to another during the terrible years, country people learned to travel great distances, and to make use of other means of transport than their legs or their oxen carts. Where these exist [West Serbia] both the male and female peasant now readily take both train and motorbus.

The peasants also learned to read newspapers. Before the war, reading a newspaper was a matter for shame: it was 'fine for gentlemen; the peasant should concentrate on his work'. The war put newspapers into the hands of the peasant, in the same way that military service introduced him to a proper bed. He would still be unlikely to read a book, still less a review. But newspapers have become familiar to him. It still seems to be impossible for him to make a regular order with regular payments, but he likes to read a newspaper from time to time. Nowadays one frequently sees a peasant woman buying a newspaper and taking it home: something quite impossible to imagine before the war.

It makes one sad to say it, but this does appear to be a truth: in the backward countries, general mobilization and war are almost the only ways of dragging them out of their old ways and inspiring change in the uncountable masses who constitute the majority of the population, of revealing in them producers who know how to work and consumers who have superior needs. But, in spite of all the individual and collective progress realized by the war to the profit of those who survived, the latter would under no circumstances wish to repeat the experience. Let us hope that future generations will find other methods for resolving their difficulties and pressing forward the chariot of progress!

(*Les effets économiques et sociaux de la guerre en Serbie*, New York, Carnegie Endowment, 1929, pp.314–15)

II.10 Entries from the journal of Brand Whitlock (1916)

August 12, 1916. – The Kelloggs here for the week-end. Kellogg's interview with von Gersky this afternoon was, I take it, somewhat reassuring.

I hear, and there seems to be no doubt of it, that Sir Roger Casement has been hanged. While technically, and from the legal standpoint, this may have been right, the action of England in reference to the whole Irish revolution is one of the most disheartening things in the present disheartening condition of the world. Waiving the question for the moment of the whole English treatment of Ireland, and it has been a series of cruel, wanton, ignorant blunders for eight centuries, one might have expected a nobler attitude from that England that pretends to be fighting, and in a way is fighting for civilization and the liberation of mankind; one might have expected some mercy from enlightened men for misguided and enthusiastic poets and scholars. Poor Ireland! But poorer England, far poorer, incapable of noble and generous action. Think what Lincoln would have done in such an emergency! But there are, alas, no Lincolns in Europe; scarcely a man in one of her chancelleries, indeed!

August 14, 1916. – The Germans have organized a *centrale* to distribute the butter, and as a result there is no more butter to be had. They have fixed a maximum price, and just as in the French Revolution, just as in every other human case where the thing has been tried – the laws of economics being so much more potent than the laws of men – there is no butter for sale! All of which shows that the human intelligence, so-called, never learns anything.

Another evidence of the reliance on law, statistics, and so on. The Germans have ordered eggs in Flanders, based on the number of hens according to their recent census. So many hens, so many eggs! Poor hens! They will have to hustle to keep out of the Kommandantur. And the pigeons! They may fly out at a certain hour, but must be back in their cotes at a given time!

August 15, 1916. – Francqui brought to our attention several letters from the Governor-General of a similar character. The Comité National gives relief to wives of Belgian officers. One woman, however, had had a baby by a German officer; and the Comité National suppressed her relief. The Governor-General rudely demanded that it be restored! There are several cases of this sort.

August 17, 1916. – One of the curious things the war has brought to Belgium is a certain liberation of women. They go out alone without chaperons; some of them walk among the poor side streets, and so forth, which many of them had never seen before. Girls ride everywhere on bicycles, there being no automobiles or other form of transport. Van Holder [a well-known painter in Brussels] says girls come and pose at his studio for their portraits; girls of the best families, without a chaperon, as they never did before the war. And Count de Jonghe made a similar observation to me the other day. Women seem to have found themselves; they work, from patriotic motives, but they work.

August 18, 1916. – A placard today announced that meat can be used, I think, only twice a week in restaurants, or that only one *plat* can be served at a meal; that cream must not be used at all, and so on. It is the beginning of the tightening of the screws – and of the belt, too. The winter will be very terrible.

(*The Letters and Journal of Brand Whitlock*, ed. Allan Nevins, East Norwalk, Conn., Appleton-Century, 1936, pp.286–7)

II.11 Report on British servants, *Bristol Evening News* (19 Feb. 1919)

Call of the home unheeded by many girls – Bristol scheme to solve problem

A meeting of employers and mistresses, arranged by the Local Advisory Committee, was held yesterday in the lesser Colston Hall, in regard to the question of domestic service in Bristol. Miss B. M. Sparks explained in opening the meeting, that it was imperative that some scheme should be evolved by which girls should be brought back to work in the homes, and to do this the conditions of domestic service must be brought into line with those of other industries, both in regarding details of conditions and wages. A draft scheme had been drawn up by the Women's Sub-Committee of the Local Advisory Committee, and it would be explained by Mr Broad, and suggestions regarding the scheme were invited.

Miss Baron pointed out that the subject was the most pressing among those affecting women's work. Women coming out of munitions industries who were in domestic service before the war showed no inclination to go back into service. That was not only the case in Bristol but all over the country, and Local Advisory Committees set up in connection with Employment Exchanges to deal with employment questions were finding everywhere that this question was most pressing. The girls' point of view must be regarded as well as the employers'. The girls had an opportunity of doing another kind of work during the war. They had more freedom, definite hours of work, and more companionship in their work. They had also felt that every bit of their work was tremendously worthwhile doing and helped in the war. They did not want to give up their freedom and companionship, or the better status they had enjoyed. To give an idea of what was happening in Bristol; there were something like 1,900 unemployed claiming donations at present, a large number of whom were probably in domestic service before the war. The Exchange had been inundated with vacancies since the meeting of domestic workers about a fortnight ago. There were 400 vacancies at present for domestics to live in, and 150 for daily workers. To show how few girls were going back to domestic service, during the four weeks ended February 7, nineteen women were placed to live in and 53 daily workers. It seemed as if something must be done to change the conditions and make domestic service more attractive. Long hours and lack of freedom were the chief objections. Various schemes had been drawn up by various bodies, one of which provided for the girls to live together in a hostel and wear a special uniform, and be under a certain amount of discipline.

Mr L. Broad [outlined] the scheme which was suggested for Bristol ... (A 'Whitley' council representing employers and employed was to be constituted and from it a root to vet prospective domestics and mistresses.)

Wages and hours. The following minimum wages would apply for resident domestics: Cooks, 21 years and upwards £30; house parlourmaids, parlourmaids and housemaids, 18 years £22, 19 years £24, 20 years £26, 21 years and upwards, £28. Generals; 18 years £20, 19 years £22, 20 years £24, 21 years and upwards £26. Between maids; 18 years £15, 19 years £20. These wages were in addition to full board and washing. The women would be given two hours daily, irrespective of meal times, a half-day holiday every week, a half-day on Sundays, and two weeks holiday a year on full wages. For meal times they would have half-hour for breakfast, one hour for dinner, and half-hour for tea. Employers would be asked to sign an agreement on these conditions, and give an assurance that the situation was a good and comfortable one, and the sleeping accommodation was satisfactory. There would be a month's notice on either side. Any complaint as to conditions of service should be referred to the weekly rota. With regard to daily and part-time workers, general work with meals would be 4d per hour (exclusive of meal times) and 6d without meals.

Criticism of the scheme was invited, and there was some discussion of details. Replying to a question as to this scheme having the effect of raising the wages of girls at present employed at lower rates, Mr Broad said the scheme might have that effect.... One lady thought such conditions would make the girl more the mistress than the employer herself ... .

(*Bristol Evening News*, 19 Feb. 1919)

II.12 Wilfred Owen, 'Strange meeting' (1918)

Preface

This book is not about heroes. English poetry is not yet fit to speak of them.

Nor is it about deeds, or lands, nor anything about glory, honour, might, majesty, dominion, or power, except War.

Above all I am not concerned with Poetry.

My subject is War, and the pity of War.

The Poetry is in the pity.

Yet these elegies are to this generation in no sense consolatory. They may be to the next. All a poet can do today is warn. That is why the true Poets must be truthful.

(If I thought the letter of this book would last, I might have used proper names; but if the spirit of it survives – survives Prussia – my ambition and those names will have achieved themselves fresher fields than Flanders ... .)

Strange Meeting

It seemed that out of battle I escaped
Down some profound dull tunnel, long since scooped
Through granites which titanic wars had groined.
Yet also there encumbered sleepers groaned,
Too fast in thought or death to be bestirred.
Then, as I probed them, one sprang up, and stared
With piteous recognition in fixed eyes,
Lifting distressful hands as if to bless.
And by his smile, I knew that sullen hall,
By his dead smile I knew we stood in Hell.
With a thousand pains that vision's face was grained;

Yet no blood reached there from the upper ground,
And no guns thumped, or down the flues made moan.
'Strange friend,' I said, 'here is no cause to mourn.'
'None,' said that other, 'save the undone years,
The hopelessness. Whatever hope is yours,
Was my life also; I went hunting wild
After the wildest beauty in the world,
Which lies not calm in eyes, or braided hair,
But mocks the steady running of the hour,
And if it grieves, grieves richlier than here.
For of my glee might many men have laughed,
And of my weeping something had been left,
Which must die now. I mean the truth untold.
The pity of war, the pity war distilled.
Now men will go content with what we spoiled,
Or, discontent, boil bloody, and be spilled.
They will be swift with swiftness of the tigress.
None will break ranks, though nations trek from progress.
Courage was mine, and I had mystery,
Wisdom was mine, and I had mastery:
To miss the march of this retreating world
Into vain citadels that are not walled.
Then, when much blood had clogged their chariot-wheels,
I would go up and wash them from sweet wells,
Even with truths that lie too deep for taint.
I would have poured my spirit without stint
But not through wounds; not on the cess of war.
Foreheads of men have bled where no wounds were.
I am the enemy you killed, my friend.
I knew you in this dark: for so you frowned
Yesterday through me as you jabbed and killed.
I parried; but my hands were loath and cold.
Let us sleep now ... .'

(Wilfred Owen, *Collected Poems*, Chatto and Windus, 1920)

II.13 Henri Barbusse, from *Under Fire* (1915)

'There are those who say,' now cries one of the sombre and compelling talkers, extending his hand as though he could see the pageant, 'there are those who say, "How fine they are!"'

'And those who say, "The nations hate each other!"'

'And those who say, "I get fat on war, and my belly matures on it!"'

'And those who say, "There has always been war, so there always will be"'

'There are those who say, "I can't see farther than the end of my nose, and I forbid others to see farther!"'

'There are those who say, "Babies come into the world with either red or blue breeches on!"'

'There are those,' growled a hoarse voice, 'who say, "Bow your head and trust in God!"'

Ah, you are right, poor countless workmen of the battles, you who have made with your hands all of the Great War, you whose omnipotence is not yet used for well-doing, you human host whose every face is a world of sorrows, you who dream bowed under the yoke of a thought beneath that sky where long black clouds rend themselves and expand in dishevelled lengths like evil angels – yes, you are right. There are all those things against you. Against you and your great common interests. which are precisely and with sacred logic blended, there are not only the sword-wavers, the profiteers, and the intriguers.

There is not only the prodigious opposition of interested parties – financiers, speculators great and small, armour-plated in their banks and houses, who live on war and live in peace during war, with their brows stubbornly set upon a secret doctrine and their faces shut up like safes.

There are those who admire the exchange of flashing blows, who hail like women the bright colours of uniforms; those whom military music and the martial ballads poured upon the public intoxicate as with brandy; the dizzy-brained, the feeble-minded, the superstitious, the savages.

There are those who bury themselves in the past, on whose lips are the sayings only of bygone days, the traditionalists for whom an injustice has legal force because it is perpetuated, who aspire to be guided by the dead, who strive to subordinate progress and the future and all their palpitating passion to the realm of ghosts and nursery-tales.

With them are all the parsons, who seek to excite you and to lull you to sleep with the morphine of their Paradise, so that nothing may change.

They pervert the most admirable of moral principles. How many are the crimes of which they have made virtues merely by dowering them with the word 'national'? They distort even truth itself. For the truth which is eternally the same they substitute each their national truth. So many nations, so many truths; and thus they falsify and twist the truth. All those people are your enemies.

They are your enemies as much as those German soldiers are to-day who are prostrate here between you in the mud, who are only poor dupes hatefully deceived and brutalised, domestic beasts. They are your enemies, wherever they were born, however they pronounce their names, whatever the language in which they lie. Look at them, in the heaven and on the earth. Look at them, everywhere! Identify them once for all, and be mindful for ever!

'They will say to you,' growled a kneeling man who stooped with his two hands in the earth and shook his shoulders like a mastiff, "My friend, you have been a wonderful hero!" I don't *want* them to say it!

'Heroes? Some sort of extraordinary being? Idols? Rot! We've been murderers. We have respectably followed the trade of murderers. We shall do it again with all our might, if we have to turn murderers again so that the real enemies can be left in peace. The act of slaughter is always ignoble; sometimes necessary, but always ignoble. Yes, hard and persistent murderers, that's what we've been. But don't talk to me about military virtue because I've killed Germans.'

'Nor to me,' cried another in so loud a voice that no one could have replied to him even had he dared; 'nor to me, because I've saved the lives of Frenchmen! Why, we might as well set fire to houses for the sake of the excellence of life-saving!'

'It would be a crime to exhibit the fine side of war, even if there were one!' murmured one of the sombre soldiers.

The first man continued. 'They'll say those things to us by way of paying us with glory, and to pay themselves, too, for what they haven't done. But military glory – it isn't even true for us common soldiers. It's for some, but outside those elect the soldier's glory is a lie, like every other fine-looking thing in war. In reality, the soldier's sacrifice is obscurely concealed. The multitudes that make up the waves of attack have no reward. They run to hurl themselves into a frightful inglorious nothing. You cannot even heap up their names, their poor little names of nobodies.'

'To hell with it all,' replies a man, 'we've got other things to think about.'

'But all that,' hiccuped a face which the mud concealed like a hideous hand, 'may you even say it? You'd be cursed, and "shot at dawn"! They've made around a Marshal's plumes a religion as bad and stupid and malignant as the other!'

The man raised himself, fell down, and rose again. The wound that he had under his armour of filth was staining the ground, and when he had spoken, his wide-open eyes looked down at all the blood he had given for the healing of the world.

The others, one by one, straighten themselves. The storm is falling more heavily on the expanse of flayed and martyred fields. The day is full of night. It is as if new hostile shapes of men and groups of men are rising unceasingly on the crest of the mountain chain of clouds, round about the barbaric outlines of crosses, eagles, churches, royal and military palaces, temples and money-markets. They seem to multiply there, shutting out the stars that are fewer than mankind; it seems even as if these apparitions are moving in all directions in the excavated ground, here, there, among the real beings who are thrown there at random, half buried in the earth like grains of corn.

My still living companions have at last got up. Standing with difficulty on the foundered soil, enclosed in their bemired garb, laid out in strange upright coffins of mud, raising their huge simplicity out of the earth's depths – a profundity like that of ignorance – they move and cry out, with their gaze, their arms and their fists extended towards the sky whence fall daylight and storm. They are struggling against victorious spectres, like the Cyranos and Don Quixotes that they still are.

One sees their shadows stirring on the shining sad expanse of the plain, and reflected in the pallid stagnant surface of the old trenches, which now only the infinite void of space inhabits and purifies, in the centre of a polar desert whose horizons fume.

But their eyes are opened. They are beginning to make out the boundless simplicity of things. And Truth not only invests them with a dawn of hope, but raises on it a renewal of strength and courage.

'That's enough talk about those others!' one of the men commanded; 'all the worse for them! – Us! Us all!' The understanding between democracies, the entente among the multitudes, the uplifting of the people of the world, the bluntly simple faith! All the rest, aye, all the rest, in the past, the present and the future, matters nothing at all.

And a soldier ventures to add this sentence, though he begins it with lowered voice, 'If the present war has advanced progress by one step, its miseries and slaughter will count for little.'

And while we get ready to rejoin the others and begin war again, the dark and storm-choked sky slowly opens above our heads. Between two masses of gloomy cloud a tranquil gleam emerges; and that line of light, so black-edged and beset, brings even so its proof that the sun is there.

(*Under Fire*, trans. W. Fitzwater-Wray, Dent, 1965, pp.339–43)

II.14 Erich Maria Remarque, from *All Quiet on the Western Front* (1929)

It is autumn. There are not many of the old hands left. I am the last of the seven fellows from our class.

Everyone talks of peace and armistice. All wait. If it again proves an illusion, then they will break up; hope is high, it cannot be taken away again without an upheaval. If there is not peace, then there will be revolution.

I have fourteen days rest, because I have swallowed a bit of gas; in the little garden I sit the whole day long in the sun. The armistice is coming soon, I believe it now too. Then we will go home.

Here my thoughts stop and will not go any farther. All that meets me, all that floods over me are but feelings – greed of life, love of home, yearning for the blood, intoxication of deliverance. But no aims.

Had we returned home in 1916, out of the suffering and the strength of our experiences we might have unleashed a storm. Now if we go back we will be weary, broken, burnt out, rootless, and without hope. We will not be able to find our way any more.

And men will not understand us – for the generation that grew up before us, though it has passed these years with us already had a home and a calling; now it will return to its old occupations, and the war will be forgotten – and the generation that has grown up after us will be strange to us and push us aside. We will be superfluous even to ourselves, we will grow older, a few will adapt themselves, some others will merely submit, and most will be bewildered; – the years will pass by and in the end we shall fall into ruin.

But perhaps all this that I think is mere melancholy and dismay, which will fly away as the dust, when I stand once again beneath the poplars and listen to the rustling of their leaves. It cannot be that it has gone, the yearning that made our blood unquiet, the unknown, the perplexing, the oncoming things, the thousand faces of the future, the melodies from dreams and from books, the whispers and divinations of women; it cannot be that this has vanished in bombardment, in despair, in brothels.

Here the trees show gay and golden, the berries of the rowan stand red among the leaves, country roads run white out to the sky line, and the canteens hum like beehives with rumours of peace.

I stand up.

I am very quiet. Let the months and years come, they can take nothing from me, they can take nothing more. I am so alone, and so without hope that I can confront them without fear. The life that has borne me through these years is still in my hands and my eyes. Whether I have subdued it, I know not. But so long as it is there it will seek its own way out, heedless of the will that is within me....

He fell in October 1918, on a day that was so quiet and still on the whole front, that the army report confined itself to the single sentence: All quiet on the Western Front.

He had fallen forward and lay on the earth as though sleeping. Turning him over one saw that he could not have suffered long; his face had an expression of calm, as though almost glad the end had come.

(*All Quiet on the Western Front*, trans. A. W. Wheen, Picador, 1987)

II.15 'The programme of the Progressive Bloc' (25 Aug. 1915)

The undersigned representatives of parties and groups in the State Council and in the State *Duma*, out of the conviction that only a strong, firm, and active authority can lead our fatherland to victory, and that such an authority can only be one supported by the confidence of the public and capable of organizing the active co-operation of all citizens, have come to the unanimous conclusion that the most essential and important task of creating such an authority cannot be realized without the fulfilment of the following conditions:

The formation of a united government, consisting of persons who enjoy the confidence of the country and are in agreement with the legislative institutions as to carrying out, at the earliest time, a definite programme; a decisive change in the methods of government hitherto employed, which have been founded on distrust of public initiative, in particular: (a) strict observance of the principle of legality in administration; (b) removal of the dual power of military and civil authority in questions that have no immediate relation to the conduct of military operations; (c) renovation of the personnel of local administration; (d) an intelligent and consistent policy directed to the maintenance of internal peace and the removal of discord between nationalities and classes.

For the realization of such a policy, the following measures must be taken in both the administrative and the legislative systems:

1. By amnesty from the Sovereign, the withdrawal of cases initiated on charges of purely political and religious offences which are not complicated by offences of a criminal character; the remission of punishment and restoration of rights, including that of taking part in elections to the State *Duma*, to *zemstvo* and town institutions, and so on, for persons condemned for such offences, and some mitigation for others who have been

condemned for political and religious offences, with the exception of spies and traitors.

2. The return of those administratively exiled for offences of a political character.
3. Full and decisive cessation of persecution for religion under any pretext whatsoever, and repeal of circulars limiting and distorting the meaning of the decree of April 17, 1905 [on religious tolerance].
4. A settlement of the Russo-Polish question, that is: repeal of limitations on the rights of Poles all over Russia, the immediate preparation and introduction into the legislative institutions of a bill on the autonomy of Russian Poland, and the simultaneous revision of the laws on Polish land ownership.
5. A beginning towards abolishing the limitations on the rights of Jews, in particular, further steps for the abolition of the Jewish Pale, facilitation of access to educational institutions, and a repeal of limitations on the choice of a profession; the restoration of the Jewish press.
6. A policy of conciliation in the Finnish question – in particular, a change in the personnel of the administration and the Senate, and the cessation of persecution of officials.
7. Restoration of the Little Russian press; the immediate review of the cases of inhabitants of Galicia kept under arrest or exiled, and the liberation of those of them who, though innocent, were subjected to prosecution.
8. The restoration of the work of trade unions, and cessation of persecution of the workers' representatives in sick benefit funds, on suspicion of belonging to an illegal party; restoration of the labour press.
9. Agreement between the government and the legislative institutions as to the speediest introduction of:
   - (a) All bills that are most closely related to national defence, the supplying of the army, the care of the wounded, the regulation of the lot of refugees, and other problems directly connected with the war.
   - (b) The following programme of legislative work, directed towards organizing the country to contribute to victory and towards the maintenance of internal peace: equalization of the rights of peasants with those of other classes; the introduction of *volost' zemstvos*; the revision of the *zemstvo* law of 1890; the revision of the municipal law of 1892; the introduction of *zemstvo* institutions in outlying areas, such as Siberia, the Archangel *guberniia* [province], the Don region, the Caucasus, and so on; bills on co-operative societies, on rest days for shop assistants, on improving the lot of postal and telegraph employees, on approving temperance forever, on *zemstvo* and town congresses and unions, on the statute concerning inspections, and on the introduction of justices of the peace in those *guberniias* where their introduction has been halted for financial reasons; and the carrying out of such legislative measures as may be found to be necessary for the administrative execution of the above described programme of action.

Signed:
For the Progressive Nationalist Group,
 V. A. Bobrinskii
For the Centre Faction,
 V. N. L'vov
For the Zermstvo-Octobrist Faction,
 I. I. Dmitriukov
For the Union of 17 October Group,
 S. I. Shidlovskii
For the Progressivist Faction,
 I. N. Efremov
For the People's Freedom [Kadet] Faction,
 P. N. Miliukov
For the Academic Group of the State Council,
 D. D. Grimm
For the Centre Group of the State Council,
 Baron V. Meller-Zakomel'skii

(George Vernadsky *et al.* (eds) *A Source Book for Russian History from Early Times to 1917*, New Haven, Conn., Yale University Press, 1972, vol. 3, pp.846–7)

II.16 Paul Miliukov, extracts from a speech in the *Duma* (1 Nov. 1916)

[Paul Miliukov was a leader of the Kadet Party.]

As heretofore, we are striving for complete victory; as heretofore, we are prepared to make all the necessary sacrifices; and, as heretofore, we are anxious to preserve our national unity. But I say this candidly: there is a difference in the situation. We have lost faith in the ability of this government to achieve victory (*Voices*: 'That's true'), because, as far as this government is concerned, neither the attempts at correction nor the attempts at improvement which we have made here have proved successful. All the Allied Powers have summoned to the ranks of their governments the very best men of all parties. They have gathered about the heads of their governments all the confidence and all those elements of organization present in their countries, which are better organized than our own. What has our own government accomplished? Our [Progressive Bloc] declaration has told that. When there was formed in the Fourth State *Duma* a majority [the Progressive Bloc] which the *Duma* had lacked theretofore, a majority ready to vote its confidence in a cabinet worthy of such confidence, then nearly all those men who might in some slight degree have been expected to receive such confidence were forced, systematically, one after another, every one of them, to leave the cabinet. And if we have formerly said that our government had neither the knowledge nor the talent necessary for the present moment, we say now, gentlemen, that this present government has sunk beneath the level on which it stood during normal times in Russian life. (*Voices on the Left*: 'True! Right!') And now the gulf between us and that government has grown wider and has become impassable.

Today we see and are aware that with this government we cannot legislate, any more than we can with this government lead Russia to victory ... We are telling this government, as the declaration of the Bloc stated: we shall fight you; we shall fight with all legitimate means until you go.... When the *Duma* with ever greater persistence insists that the rear must be organized for a successful struggle, while the government persists in claiming that organizing the country means organizing a revolution and deliberately prefers chaos and disorganization, then what is this: stupidity or treason? (*A voice on the Left*: 'Treason!' *Adzhemov*: 'Stupidity!' *Laughter.*) ...

You must realize, also, why we, too, have no task left to us today other than that which I have already pointed out: to obtain the resignation of this government ... We have many, very many, separate reasons for being dissatisfied with the government. If we have time, we shall speak of them. But all these particular reasons boil down to this general one: the government, as presently composed, is incapable and ill intentioned. (*Voices on the Left*: 'Correct!') This is the main evil, a victory over which will be tantamount to winning the whole campaign.

(George Vernadsky *et al.* (eds) *A Source Book for Russian History from Early Times to 1917*, New Haven, Conn., Yale University Press, 1972, vol. 3, p.870)

II.17 Nicholai Markov, extract from a speech in the *Duma* (3 Nov. 1916)

[Markov was a member of the right-wing Union of the Russian People.]

If the people and the workers believe your words ... then ... be aware that the people and the workers are men of action, men with toil-hardened hands; they are not windbags, and, unfortunately, they do believe your words; and if you say 'we shall fight against government authority during this terrible war,' then realize that this means that the workers would strike, that they would raise the banner of revolt; and do not hide behind the pretence that you wish to confine yourself to words alone. No, be aware that your words will lead to revolt, to rebellion, to an insurrection of the people, to a weakening of the state at a time when the state is trembling from the blows of a hateful, evil, despicable enemy.

Gentlemen, you apparently do not realize what you wish to accomplish, so I shall explain it to you: you wish to bring on a revolution in Russia so that a revolution would destroy the entire Russian state, well formed or not.

(George Vernadsky *et al.* (eds) *A Source Book for Russian History from Early Times to 1917*, New Haven, Conn., Yale University Press, 1972, vol. 3, pp.870–1)

II.18 Vladimir Purishkevich, extract from a speech in the *Duma* (19 Nov. 1916)

[Purishkevich was founder of the Union of the Russian People.]

Gentlemen, I mount this tribune today with inexpressible emotional agitation, and not because I have left the ranks of my faction. I cannot abandon the ranks of the Right, for I am perhaps the Right-most of all those who are in the Right camp. But there are moments, gentlemen ...when one cannot allow oneself to speak from the bell tower of an *uezd* or *guberniia* town but must ring the alarm from the bell tower of Ivan the Great [in the Kremlin in Moscow] ... Today, as formerly and in the future, there burns within me an infinite love for my native land and a selfless, boundless, and most devoted allegiance to my sovereign. I am living at this moment with but a single thought – that of a Russian victory. But today, as before, I have within me no slavish obsequiousness before the organs of the ruling power, and I could not enter my name as a member of the ministerial antechamber. (*Applause in the Centre and on the Left. Voices in the Centre:* 'Bravo!') I clearly see, gentlemen, who and what it is that is harming Russia, impeding her, and postponing the hour of her certain victory over the external enemy.

The disorganization of our rear is undoubtedly being carried out by the enemy, and it is being done by a strong, relentless, and resolute hand. We have a single system, the system of devastation in the rear. This system was set up by Wilhelm himself and is being carried out by him with amazing consistency with the aid of the German party working in our rear.

What today, gentlemen, is the principal scourge of Russian public and official life? Here are four propositions: the first is the senseless censorship of that which ought not to be censored; the second is the hypocrisy and paralysis of the government; the third is the dangerous symptoms of the triumph of Germanophile tendencies among the organs of the government; and, in connection with this, the fourth is absolute uncertainty as to the morrow, with new government policies cooked up from day to day.

I take the liberty to say here, from the rostrum of the State *Duma*, that all this evil comes from those dark forces, from those influences which push this or that individual into position and which force up into high posts people who are not capable of filling them, from those influences headed by Grishka Rasputin ... It is necessary that the legislative body, being the voice of the entire country and now united in spirit on the question of victory, finally raise its voice about this, Russia's greatest evil, which is corrupting Russian public life. These past nights I couldn't sleep, I give you my word of honour. I lie with eyes open and imagine a series of telegrams, reports, notes which this illiterate peasant writes now to one minister, then to another, and most frequently of all, it is said, to Aleksandr Dmitrievich Protopopov,[7] and which he requests them to act upon. And we know there were instances when the failure to fulfil these demands entailed the fall of these strong and powerful men ....

I shall take the liberty of addressing now the Council of Ministers, quite apart from the *Duma*, whose duty I have already indicated. If the ministers consider duty above career – and I believe that at this moment duty is above career – and if you really are a united cabinet, then go to the tsar and say that things cannot go on any longer in this way. This is not a boycott of authority, gentlemen, but your duty before the sovereign. If you are loyal to your sovereign, if the glory of Russia, her power, her future, intimately and inseparably bound up with the grandeur and splendour of the tsar's name, are dear to you, go to Imperial Head-

[7] Protopopov was the last tzarist minister of the interior appointed in September 1916 on the insistence of the Tzarina and on the advice of Rasputin. Protopopov was believed to have made peace overtures to Germany.

quarters, throw yourselves at the tsar's feet, and beg permission to open his eyes to the dreadful reality, beg him to deliver Russia from Rasputin and the Rasputinites both big and small....

Gentlemen, we must plead with the sovereign, and you (*turning to the ministers*), his loyal servants, chosen to carry out his will, you, primarily responsible for the course of the Russian ship of state, united with us, go to headquarters and plead with the sovereign that Grishka Rasputin not be the leader of Russian internal public life. (*Loud and prolonged applause from the Centre, Left, and Right; voices*: 'Bravo!')

(George Vernadsky *et al.* (eds) *A Source Book for Russian History from Early Times to 1917*, New Haven, Conn., Yale University Press, 1972, vol. 3, pp.872–3)

II.19 'The Proclamation of the Provisional Government' (1 March 1917)

From the provisional government

Citizens!

The Provisional Committee of members of the State *Duma*, with the aid and sympathy of the troops and the population of the capital, has at present scored such a degree of success over the dark forces of the old regime that it can now proceed to a more durable organization of executive power.

To this end, the Provisional Committee of the State *Duma* appoints as ministers of the first public [*obshchestvennyi*] cabinet the following persons, the country's confidence in whom is guaranteed by their past public and political activities.

Chairman of the Council of Ministers and Minister of Internal Affairs: Prince G. E. L'vov

Minister of Foreign Affairs: P. N. Miliukov
Minister of War and the Navy: A. I. Guchkov
Minister of Means of Communications: N. V. Nekrasov
Minister of Trade and Industry: A. I. Konovalov
Minister of Public Education: A. A. Manuilov
Minister of Finance: M. I. Tereshchenko
Chief Procurator of the Holy Synod: V. N. L'vov
Minister of Agriculture: A. I. Shingarev
Minister of justice: A. F. Kerenskii
State Comptroller: I. V. Godnev
Minister for Finnish Affairs: F. I. Rodichev

The Cabinet will be guided in its present activity by the following principles:

1. Full and immediate amnesty in all political and religious cases, including terrorist attempts, military uprisings and agrarian offences, and so forth.
2. Freedom of speech, the press, unions, assembly, and strikes, with the extension of political freedoms to servicemen within limits permitted by military and technical conditions.

3. Abolition of all class, religious, and national restrictions.
4. Immediate preparations for the convocation – on the basis of universal, equal, direct, and secret suffrage – of a constituent assembly which will establish the form of government and the constitution of the country.
5. Replacement of the police by a people's militia with an elected command, subordinate to the organs of local self-government.
6. Elections to the organs of local self-government on the basis of universal, direct, equal, and secret ballot.
7. Non-disarmament and non-transfer from Petrograd of the military units that participated in the revolutionary movement.
8. Along with the preservation of strict military discipline in the ranks and during performance of military duty, the abolition of all restrictions upon the soldiers' enjoyment of those public rights that have been granted to all other citizens. The Provisional Government considers it its duty to add that it by no means intends to use the military situation to delay in any way the realization of the above reforms and measures.

Chairman of the State *Duma* M. V. Rodzianko
Chairman of the Council of Ministers Prince G. E. L'vov
Ministers: P. N. Miliukov, N. V. Nekrasov, A. I. Konovalov, A. A. Manuilov, M. I. Tereshchenko, Vl. N. L'vov, A. I. Shingarev, A. F. Kerenskii

(George Vernadsky *et al.* (eds) *A Source Book for Russian History from Early Times to 1917*, New Haven, Conn., Yale University Press, 1972, vol. 3, pp.881–2)

II.20 'Order No. 1' (1 March 1917) from The Petrograd Soviet of Workers and Soldiers' Deputies

To the garrison of the Petrograd *okrug*, to all the soldiers of the guard, army, artillery, and navy, for immediate and strict execution, and to the workers of Petrograd for their information:

The Soviet of Workers' and Soldiers' Deputies has resolved:

1. In all companies, battalions, regiments, parks, batteries, squadrons, in the special services of the various military administrations, and on the vessels of the navy, committees of elected representatives from the lower ranks of the above-mentioned military units shall be chosen immediately.
2. In all those military units that have not yet chosen their representatives to the Soviet of Workers' Deputies, one representative from each company shall be selected, to report with written credentials at the building of the State *Duma* by ten o'clock in the morning of the third of this March.
3. In all its political activities the military branch is subordinated to the Soviet of Workers' and Soldiers' Deputies and to its own committees.

4. The orders of the military commission of the State *Duma* shall be executed only in such cases as they do not conflict with the orders and resolutions of the Soviet of Workers' and Soldiers' Deputies.
5. All kinds of arms, such as rifles, machine guns, armoured automobiles and others, must be kept at the disposal and under the control of the company and battalion committees and must in no case be turned over to officers, even at their demand.
6. In the ranks and during their performance of the duties of the service, soldiers must observe the strictest military discipline, but outside the service and the ranks, in their political, general civic, and private lives, soldiers cannot in any way be deprived of those rights that all citizens enjoy. In particular, standing at attention and compulsory saluting, when not on duty, are abolished.
7. Also, the addressing of the officers with the titles 'Your Excellency,' 'Your Honour,' and the like, is abolished, and these titles are replaced by the address of 'Mister General,' 'Mister Colonel,' and so forth. Rudeness towards soldiers of any rank, and, especially, addressing them as 'thou,' is prohibited, and soldiers are required to bring to the attention of the company committees every infraction of this rule, as well as all misunderstandings occurring between officers and enlisted men.

The present order is to be read to all companies, battalions, regiments, ships' crews, batteries, and other combatant and non-combatant commands.

The Petrograd Soviet of Workers' and Soldiers' Deputies

(George Vernadsky *et al.* (eds) *A Source Book for Russian History from Early Times to 1917*, New Haven, Conn., Yale University Press, 1972, vol. 3, p.882).

II.21 'Declaration of the Kronstadt soldiers' (1 March 1921)

Having heard the report of the representatives sent by the general meeting of ships' crews to Petrograd to investigate the situation there, we resolve:

1. In view of the fact that the present soviets do not express the will of the workers and peasants, immediately to hold new elections by secret ballot, with freedom to carry on agitation beforehand for all workers and peasants;
2. To give freedom of speech and press to workers and peasants, to anarchists and left socialist parties;
3. To secure freedom of assembly for trade unions and peasant organizations;

4. To call a non-party conference of the workers, Red Army soldiers, and sailors of Petrograd, Kronstadt, and Petrograd province, no later than March 10, 1921;
5. To liberate all political prisoners of socialist parties, as well as all workers, peasants, soldiers, and sailors imprisoned in connection with the labour and peasant movements;
6. To elect a commission to review the cases of those being held in prisons and concentration camps;
7. To abolish all political departments because no party should be given special privileges in the propagation of its ideas or receive the financial support of the state for such purposes. Instead, there should be established cultural and educational commissions, locally elected and financed by the state;
8. To remove immediately all roadblock detachments;
9. To equalize the rations of all working people, with the exception of those employed in trades detrimental to health;
10. To abolish the Communist fighting detachments in all branches of the army, as well as the Communist guards kept on duty in factories and mills. Should such guards or detachments be found necessary, they are to be appointed in the army from the ranks and in the factories and mills at the discretion of the workers;
11. To give the peasants full freedom of action in regard to the land, and also the right to keep cattle, on condition that the peasants manage with their own means, that is, without employing hired labour;
12. To request all branches of the army, as well as our comrades the military cadets (*kursanty*), to endorse our resolution;
13. To demand that the press give all our resolutions wide publicity;
14. To appoint an itinerant bureau of control;
15. To permit free handicrafts production by one's own labour.

Petrichenko, Chairman of the Squadron Meeting
Perepelkin, Secretary

(Paul Avrich, *Kronstadt 1921*, Princeton University Press, 1970, pp.73–4)

II.22 'Kronstadt sailors' appeal' (8 March 1921)

What we are fighting for

After carrying out the October Revolution, the working class had hoped to achieve its emancipation. But the result was an even greater enslavement of the human personality. The power of the police and gendarme monarchy passed into the hands of the Communist usurpers, who, instead of giving the people freedom, instilled in them the constant fear of falling into the torture chambers of the *Cheka*, which in their horrors far exceed the gendarme administration of the tsarist regime. The bayonets, bullets, and gruff commands of the *Cheka oprichniki* – these are what the working man of Soviet Russia has won after so much struggle and suffering. The glorious emblem of the workers' state – the sickle and hammer – has in fact been replaced by the Communist authorities with the bayonet and barred window, for the sake of maintaining the calm and carefree life of the new bureaucracy of Communist commissars and functionaries.

But most infamous and criminal of all is the moral servitude which the Communists have inaugurated: they have laid their hands also on the inner world of the toilers, forcing them to think in the Communist way. With the help of the bureaucratized trade unions, they have fastened the workers to their benches, so that labour has become not a joy but a new form of slavery. To the protests of the peasants, expressed in spontaneous uprisings, and those of the workers, whose living conditions have driven them out on strike, they answer with mass executions and bloodletting, in which they have not been surpassed even by the tsarist generals. Russia of the toilers, the first to raise the red banner of labour's emancipation, is drenched in the blood of those martyred for the glory of Communist domination. In this sea of blood, the Communists are drowning all the great and glowing pledges and watchwords of the workers' revolution. The picture has been drawn more and more sharply, and now it is clear that the Russian Communist party is not the defender of the toilers that it pretends to be. The interests of the working people are alien to it. Having gained power, it is afraid only of losing it, and therefore deems every means permissible: slander, violence, deceit, murder, vengeance upon the families of the rebels.

The long-suffering patience of the toilers is at an end. Here and there the land is lit up by the fires of insurrection in a struggle against oppression and violence. Strikes by the workers have flared up, but the Bolshevik *okhrana* agents have not been asleep and have taken every measure to forestall and suppress the inevitable third revolution. But it has come nevertheless. and it is being made by the hands of the toilers themselves. The generals of Communism see clearly that it is the people who have risen, convinced that the ideas of socialism have been betrayed. Yet, trembling for their skins and aware that there is no escape from the wrath of the workers, they still try, with the help of their *oprichniki*, to terrorize the rebels with prison, firing-squads, and other atrocities. But life under the yoke of the Communist dictatorship has become more terrible than death.

The rebellious working people understand that there is no middle ground in the struggle against the Communists and the new serfdom that they have erected. One must go on to the end. They give the appearance of making concessions: in Petrograd province roadblock detachments have been removed and 10 million gold rubles have been allotted for the purchase of foodstuffs from abroad. But one must not be deceived, for behind this bait is concealed the iron hand of the master, the dictator, who aims to be repaid a hundred-fold for his concessions once calm is restored.

No, there can be no middle ground. Victory or death! The example is being set by Red Kronstadt, menace of counterrevolutionaries of the right and of the left. Here the new revolutionary step forward has been taken. Here is raised the banner of rebellion against the three-year-old violence and oppression of Communist rule, which has put in the shade the three-hundred-year yoke of monarchism. Here in Kronstadt has been laid the first stone of the third revolution, striking the last fetters from the labouring masses and opening a broad new road for socialist creativity.

The new revolution will also rouse the labouring masses of the East and of the West, by serving as an example of the new socialist construction as opposed to the bureaucratic Communist 'creativity'. The labouring masses abroad will see with their own eyes that everything created here until now by the will of the workers and peasants was not socialism. Without a single shot, without a drop of blood, the first step has been taken. The toilers do not need blood. They will shed it only at a moment of self-defence. In spite of all the outrageous acts of the Communists, we have enough restraint to confine ourselves only to isolating them from public life so that their malicious and false agitation will not hinder our revolutionary work.

The workers and peasants steadfastly march forward, leaving behind them the Constituent Assembly, with its bourgeois regime, and the dictatorship of the Communist party, with its *Cheka* and its state capitalism, whose hangman's noose encircles the necks of the labouring masses and threatens to strangle them to death. The present overturn at last gives the toilers the opportunity to have their freely elected soviets, operating without the slightest force of party pressure, and to remark the bureaucratized trade unions into free associations of workers, peasants, and the labouring intelligentsia. At last the policeman's club of the Communist autocracy has been broken.

(Paul Avrich, *Kronstadt 1921*, Princeton University Press, 1970, pp.241–3)

II.23 'The *Reichstag* resolution of 19 July 1917'

The *Reichstag* strives for a peace of understanding and the permanent reconciliation of peoples. Forced territorial acquisitions and political, economic, or financial oppressions are irreconcilable with such a peace. The *Reichstag* also rejects all plans which aim at economic isolation and hostility among nations after the war. The freedom of the seas must be made secure. Only an economic peace will prepare the ground for a friendly intercourse between the nations. The *Reichstag* will strongly promote the creation of international judicial organizations. However, as long as the enemy governments will not enter upon such a peace, as long as they threaten Germany and her allies with conquests and coercion, the German nation will stand together as a man and steadfastly hold out and fight until its own and its allies' right to life and development is secured. The German nation is invincible in its unity. The *Reichstag* knows that in this respect it is in harmony with the men who in heroic struggle are defending the Fatherland. The imperishable gratitude of the whole people is assured them.

(Gerald D. Feldman (ed.) *German Imperialism 1914–1918: The Development of a Historical Debate*, New York, Wiley, 1972, p.42)

II.24 Extract from the diary of Hans Peter Hanssen (Nov. 1918)

[Hanssen was a *Reichstag* deputy representing North Schleswig, a province with a large Danish minority that had been taken from Denmark by the war of 1864. Hanssen was spokesman for the Danish minority during the war, which brought him into close contact with the SPD and especially with critics and opponents of the war. Following a plebiscite in 1920, much of Schleswig was returned to Denmark.]

Berlin, November 3, 1918. It is Sunday. At noon I was in the *Reichstag*. From the windows of the reading room I saw that a demonstration was taking place at Bismarck's statue. I went out on the balcony to hear the speeches. The Pan-Germans were giving a demonstration. They were passionately urging that peace negotiations be broken off and that the struggle be continued to the end. Patriotic songs were sung between speeches: *Deutschland, Deutschland, Die Wacht am Rhein, Heil Dir im Siegerkranz.* A noncommissioned officer jumped up on the pedestal and protested against the continuation of the war. The people became enraged. The police stepped in and carried him away.

As I was coming through the Siegesallee, a man fell unconscious directly in front of me. With the help of a passerby, I lifted him up on the pedestal beside the tomb of Kaiser Wilhelm. When he had regained consciousness, he whispered: 'Haven't had anything to eat since yesterday.' He was emaciated and half-dead from hunger. We saw to it that he received help.

There is much unrest in the working quarters. The Social Democratic press is using unusually sharp language against the Kaiser. Noske's articles in the *Chemnitzer Volksstimme* are helpful for the information they give. If the Kaiser does not abdicate soon, the Majority Socialists will be in a very difficult position.

On the whole it looks like a storm. While I was eating at Kempinski's this evening, I was seated at a table near two young men. They talked about the war. 'During the first year we were pleasantly led around by the nose,' said one bitterly. 'After being in the war for thirty-seven months without interruption,' said the other, 'my nerves are completely wrecked. I really live only when I can get alcohol. I have now only one desire: I was born a human being and want to be treated like a human being. But during the past four years I have been treated like an animal.'

A well-dressed gentleman and lady came and took a seat beside us. The gentleman joined in the conversation immediately. It turned out that he was a Rheinlander and had, like the others, participated in the war as a reserve officer. He had been severely wounded by a bullet which had gone straight through his head. 'Life is over for me,' he said indifferently; 'I now live only when I am drunk. The Kaiser ought to be shot and the military abolished! If a battle is called for that purpose, I'll go at once. One would have an opportunity to fight for a righteous cause.' The others eagerly gave their approval to the remark. When I expressed my astonishment at this strong language, they said to each other: 'That's the general attitude. In South Germany, it is much worse!'

Berlin, November 7, 1918. This morning, when I went to the *Reichstag* by a roundabout way, the streets presented a very warlike scene. Troops were marching in field equipment with shiny steel helmets. Street corners were occupied by strong military posts. Wherever it was possible to use a street strategically, windows in the upper stories of the buildings were dotted with machine guns. I passed several batteries. The artillery drove through the streets and made it plain that the cannon were ready for action, in order to show the citizens of Berlin what they may count on if they revolt. There is a foreshadowing of a bloody struggle ... .

About five o'clock I returned to the *Reichstag*, where I met Ledebour.[8] 'You here?' I said, 'I thought you were at Kiel.'

He: 'No, we must divide up. We must also have people here in town.'

I: 'How are things going today?'

He: 'Kiel, Rendsburg, Hamburg, Lübeck, and Schwerin are in our hands. We are in control in Schleswig-Holstein, Mecklenburg, and the Hanse cities, but we will go further.'

I: 'What actually happened in Kiel?'

He: 'The Great Fleet was about to make an advance. The sailors declared: "We refuse to go. We will defend ourselves, but we will not attack under present conditions." Several hundred sailors were then arrested. The stokers on several ships put the fires out, and the sailors assumed control. The situation at Kiel, however, is still difficult, because the press, party officers, and the organizations still remain in the Government's socialist camp.'

I: 'What about things here?'

He: 'Our meeting tonight is forbidden, but that will only spread oil on the flames.'

I: 'Will anything happen tonight?'

He: 'No, we will not do anything. That would only cause deaths to no advantage. But we will soon have the upper hand. At a meeting which we held in Berlin last night I asked the gathering to drink to long life for the revolutionists, those brave seamen at Kiel. Scarcely had I made this request when the police lieutenant jumped up and broke up the meeting. I replied by shouting to the gathering: "The meeting is not dissolved; let us continue!" Then the police lieutenant laid hands on me and said: "You are under arrest; you will immediately come with me to headquarters!" "No!" I replied, "I shall go home when the meeting is over," and turned to the gathering: "Will some of you see to it that the lieutenant remains quiet while we proceed!" Many immediately assumed a threatening attitude, and a few men with clenched fists jumped up on the platform. This was sufficient. The lieutenant remained calm, and we resumed the proceedings. When I ended the meeting, he became courageous again and said: "You are under arrest, you will follow me to headquarters!" "No," I replied, "I will not follow you; I'm going home." And then to the audience: "Will you see that the gentleman remains here until I am gone?" I left the meeting, and the police did not dare to lay hands on me. In the meantime I did not go home, and it was a good thing that I didn't since the police came to my residence shortly afterwards to arrest me. Instead, I came here to the *Reichstag*, where they dare not violate my immunity.

'Thus we will go on. The police can support itself only upon a tottering authority. It no longer has any genuine power. And what authority it has left will soon be destroyed. We speak as we wish, and the guards see to it that the police

[8] (George Ledebour, SPD journalist and editor, member of the Reichstag.

will not touch us, and that we can again leave our quarters without being molested.

'The situation will now quickly come to a head. The revolution is marching in seven league boots. The socialist republic will soon be proclaimed. There is no other way out.'

(*Diary of a Dying Empire*, Port Washington, New York, Kennikat Press, 1973, pp.339–40, 342–4)

II.25 From a report by Herr von Tschirschky, German Ambassador in Vienna (Sept. 1916)

The longer the war lasts, the more strongly the simple question whether Austria-Hungary will be able to carry on the fight, not only in the military but also in the economic field, comes to the foreground ....

The reserves of troops are nearly exhausted, and we should expect that next spring Austria-Hungary will reach the limit of its military potential, though perhaps not in the sphere of production of armaments and ammunition, where surprising progress has been made under our leadership. The mood of depression here is increased – unfortunately not without justification – by the economic situation. This and the political measures concerning economy are simply impossible. There is no organization; when attempts were made to organize after our example, they ran into difficulties because of the local proclivity for 'muddling through', and because of an economy based on protection. No systematic work in this respect has been done, regulations were made without expert knowledge, and usually for one province at a time: such practices have led to a completely unjust distribution of provisions. The people in the suburbs of Vienna are starving; they are driven to despair by long queueing, which often brings no results ... The situation has become still more serious since the poor results of this year's harvest in Austria and in Hungary, and also by the unsatisfactory economic relations between the two countries, which should, and this goes especially for Hungary, support each other loyally with food supplies. The Hungarian government, led by Count Tisza, pursues a Hungarian policy; in spite of high-minded phrases, it has no understanding of common needs and aims. Here, too, there is no personality that could dictate a policy which would safeguard common interests ....

I would like to point out that during the war, the relations between the two parts of the monarchy have deteriorated considerably. Although the feeling of common interest had seemed, at the beginning of the war, to have been strengthened by common danger, some time later exactly the opposite happened. Hungary in trying to loosen its ties with Austria more than ever before. Hungarian chauvinism is flourishing and one must admit that this is mainly Austria's fault. The many mistakes made by the Supreme Command – which is exclusively in Austrian hands – has embittered the Hungarians. The sins of Vienna's internal policy, committed during several decades, which have made the treason of the Czechs possible and for which many Hungarians have died, have also had their effect on the people in Hungary .... Magyar regiments are stationed in Bohemia in order to prevent unrest there, instead of being able to defend their fatherland. Recently, an Austrian politician has told me: 'Bohemia is in fact occupied by the Hungarians. 'Nobody in Austria is prepared to introduce a new policy in the Czech lands: this was further illustrated when both the Czech members of the cabinet, who are ministers not because of their qualifications but because they represent their people, were elevated to the rank of baron....

A similar [i.e. chaotic] situation can be observed in the financial field. Although the Minister of Finance has the best intentions of introducing order, he despairs because he cannot make the two Premiers introduce suitable measures. Germany pays its ally 100,000,000 marks every month, and apart from that it transfers to Austria regular subsidies for Bulgaria and Turkey; it is not impossible that the monarchy will present to us further bills in order to maintain the value of its currency....

I believe that we should make an attempt to stabilize the situation here. We are running the danger that the Habsburg monarchy will suddenly sicken, and that Germany will share in its downfall.

(*The Break-up of the Habsburg Empire 1914–1918: A Study in National and Social Revolution*, Oxford University Press, 1961, pp.96–7)